Creating the
HANDS-ON
MANAGER

Creating the
HANDS-ON MANAGER

The Complete Management
Development Guide

BILL WATTS

with Alison Corke

MERCURY BOOKS
Published by
W.H. Allen & Co Plc
London

First published in 1988
by the Mercury Books Division of
W.H. Allen & Co. Plc
44 Hill Street, London W1X 8LB

Set in Concorde and Helvetica by Phoenix Photosetting, Chatham
Printed and bound in Great Britain

Edited by Peter Drew
Design by Cecil Smith

ISBN 1 85251 080 3

DEAR CHIEF EXECUTIVE

There are books that tell you how to be an effective manager in a minute. There are also books that tell you how to make your organisation successful by copying what excellent organisations do. The problem with these books, as you have probably already discovered, lies in trying to follow their recommendations. They just don't seem to fit the realities of your organisation and its operating environment.

So how do you improve your organisation's performance and make your manager more effective? Well, you are invited to find out by using this book. Creating the 'hands on' manager is designed not just to tell your managers what they should be doing, it is designed to show them how to improve their performance in a way best suited to your organisation.

The book works by taking your managers back to basics and then helping them to build in the essentials for long-term efficiency and effectiveness in their specific jobs.

Consider, for a moment, the organisations you know that are successful. Whatever they do, or however large or small they are, you are likely to find that they all have two things in common. Firstly, they are structured for the environments in which they operate and want to operate. Secondly, they are staffed by efficient and effective managers. That is, managers who are really pro-active and who are controlling the course of events. Good management is the difference that makes success possible.

This book does not introduce your managers to any magic formulas or quick solutions. It does, however, provide them with sound practical advice, that is, advice based on hard, empirical research. If your managers follow the development processes in this book, in the recommended way, your organisation will become both more efficient and more effective.

This invitation is extended to you personally because the commitment to improving managerial performance should come from the top. Only with your personal overt co-operation and involvement can the maximum potential of the approaches in this book be realised.

Bill Watts

WHAT IS A HANDS-ON MANAGER?

The 'hands on' manager is one who manages when and where it counts. A manager who is appropriate for the thinking workers of the 1980/90s, an organisational front runner who provides the dynamic direction for employees' efforts. 'Hands on' managers get results and achieve organisation objectives by:

(1) STIMULATING not THREATENING The performance of the team will be maximised by their approach. They motivate team members by helping them achieve personal objectives while they contribute to the team's tasks. They realise that threatened people give the minimum they can.

(2) GUIDING not IMPOSING Team members are happy seeking their guidance in deciding the best way forward. They know that there is more than one right way to successful task completion. They realise that imposing too many rules on what people do simply reduces progress to one pace, that of the slowest.

(3) ENCOURAGING not RESTRICTING People grow and develop under their management. They encourage their people to solve their own problems and take responsibility for their own actions. They allow their team members to show initiative and reward them for doing so. They are aware that restricting people reduces and finally kills off their willingness to contribute to the organisation's goals.

(4) PRO-ACTING not RE-ACTING They do not wait for things to happen, they make things happen. They are constantly seeking opportunities to move forward and respond to new challenges. Team members know that their pro-active approach maximises opportunities and reduces unpleasant surprises. They realise that re-actors always end up dancing to someone else's tune.

(5) CREATING not PERPETUATING They use innovation to stop the organisation stagnating. They are always looking for better ways to do things and never allow systems to become ends in themselves. Team members know that they can be creative under their management and that they will act as champions for their ideas. They are aware that creativity is the rich soil from which both their team and their organisation grow.

(6) FACILITATING not PROCRASTINATING They use their position to facilitate progress. They manage by exception not procrastination. Their teams know that they can rely on them to open doors, make prompt decisions and support team members' actions. They appreciate the value of decisiveness and the frustration and demotivation of long, drawn out procedures. Red tape does not exist around these managers.

'Hands on' managers are the basic ingredient of organisational success.

CONTENTS

3. MEASURING MANAGERIAL PERFORMANCE 70

4. BUILDING THE MANAGEMENT TEAM 102

5. STRATEGIES, STRUCTURES AND SYSTEMS 123

6. MANAGING LEADERSHIP   146

APPENDIXES   169

1

DEFINING MANAGEMENT TASKS

TASKS AND TIME

Management is a discipline in its own right, just the same as engineering or nursing. Unfortunately it is often treated as an appendage to an individual's previously acquired specialism, a status indicator and no more. Those who are placed in management positions for the first time often find the transition very difficult and wish they had been better prepared for the task. Although the title 'manager' may be easy to acquire, the skills needed to manage effectively are not. To become an effective manager takes time and planned development. That process begins with the identification of the manager's key tasks.

Managing is an activity carried out under constant pressure. A typical manager's day is one of fragmented activities with attention having to be switched, on average, every nine minutes. In such circumstances the use of time becomes crucial, yet many managers do not know how best to use this valuable resource. To use time effectively is the first step towards success in management.

This chapter considers the need for management, the key activities of the manager and how managers can use their time more effectively. Carefully designed discovery exercises will enable you and your managers to get to grips with the discipline of management. By the end of the chapter you will understand how much more effective management could be in your organisation. At that point the first two objectives in the process of developing a 'hands on' management team will have been achieved. They are:

TO IDENTIFY THE CRITICAL ACTIVITIES OF EACH MAN-
AGER AND TO EXPAND THE TIME AVAILABLE FOR
MANAGING.

The Need For Management

All organisations are formed for a purpose; usually the members wish to achieve certain common goals and objectives. To do this they have to decide who does what, when and how. Management starts when specific members are assigned to tasks related to making and actioning these decisions. As organisations expand new goals and objectives are sought, organisational functions become more complex and managerial responsibilities increase.

Organisational survival and the continued achievement of objectives largely depend on the development and maintenance of functional efficiency. In some operating environments it is possible for organisations to function well below their potential. In most operating environments, however, commercial realities ruthlessly expose functional inadequacies. Organisations faced with such situations have just two choices: change, so as to function properly, or cease to exist.

Management is needed to see that an organisation functions properly. It is the component of the organisation that is responsible for mobilising and deploying people, resources and money in a way that enables it to go on achieving objectives. In essence management is the necessary catalyst that welds an organisation into an effective force. If management fails then so will the organisation.

Is It Managing?

The main tasks of managing are not as complex as the job itself but they do need to be fully understood. Perhaps the best way to start the process of developing and improving your manager's effectiveness is by asking them the question 'Is it managing?' in relation to a number of questions, statements and policies.

Use the questionnaire in Development Guide 1 for this purpose. Allowing no longer than fifteen minutes ask your managers to complete the questionnaire. When they have finished use the remaining pages of the development guide to discuss their responses. Watch for scores under 15: these indicate there is room for improvement; scores under 10 should be viewed with concern.

DISCOVERY EXERCISE

Is it Managing?   *Allow 15 minutes.*

Is it Managing?

DEVELOPMENT GUIDE 1

NAME: _____ DATE: _____

TASK ONE Read the questions listed 1 to 10. Decide how you as a manager would respond and then put an **X** in the appropriate column.

	YES	NO	NOT SURE
(1) The initial screening interviews for a vacancy in your department are being arranged. Should you plan to attend?			
(2) You have received a request from another department to accompany one of your team to assist them in solving a client's technical problem. Do you try to go?			
(3) One of your new team members has asked you for your solution to an old and recurring problem. Do you **(YES)** tell them the solution or **(NO)** expect them to find the solution themselves by tackling the problem?			
(4) One of your experienced team members has encountered a new problem which they want to discuss with you. Should you **(YES)** give them your ideas for a solution or **(NO)** wait to hear what they recommend?			
(5) You believe another department could help solve a problem one of your team has been given the task of solving. Should you contact the other department?			
(6) If one of your team members has earned a bonus for extra performance, would you personally explain to them the reasons?			
(7) Your organisation has been approached by a local university who want someone to give a talk on your department's work to a group of business studies undergraduates. Should you as the manager give the talk?			
(8) Your departmental facilities need to be reorganised and planned. Should you draw up the plans detailing where everything is to go?			
(9) You have an idea which is likely to affect the work of some of your team members. Should you **(YES)** discuss it with the members before taking it further or **(NO)** finalise the details and then carefully explain the idea to them?			
(10) One of your team members has failed to apply themselves to an urgent task. Do you **(YES)** give the task to another team member or **(NO)** discuss the situation with them to improve their performance?			

Is it Managing?

DEVELOPMENT GUIDE 1

TASK TWO Read the statements 11 to 15. Decide how you as a manager would respond and then put an **X** in the appropriate column.

	YES	NO	NOT SURE
(11) Before a new method of working is introduced in a department the manager should call a meeting to discuss the situation and agree how the changes will be introduced.			
(12) Seminars and conferences on technical developments related to the work of a department should be attended by the departmental manager.			
(13) Even if it is only by telephone, it's important for managers to discuss their progress with their boss once a week.			
(14) If important people visit a department the manager should normally show them around.			
(15) Before actually starting on the departmental budget, a manager should discuss with the team the major items of expenditure that are likely for the coming year.			

TASK THREE Read the policies 16 to 20. Decide how you as a manager would respond and then put an **X** in the appropriate column.

	YES	NO	NOT SURE
(16) It is your organisation's policy that managers see and sign all the cheques and forms related to their team's routine expenditures and requisitions. Do you agree with this policy?			
(17) It is your organisation's policy that all the paperwork related to the service pay rises of a team is personally dealt with by the team's manager. **Do you agree with this policy?**			
(18) It is your organisation's policy that all managers prepare and present their departmental budgets to senior management. **Do you agree with this policy?**			
(19) It is your organisation's policy that the progress of key team members towards their agreed objectives by reviewed by their managers each month. Each member is required to provide a written progress report. **Do you agree with this policy?**			
(20) It is your organisation's policy that once a budget is agreed by senior management it is fixed for the year and no one can change it. **Do you agree with this policy?**			

Is it Managing?   DEVELOPMENT GUIDE 1

NOTES FOR DISCUSSION I suggest that each question, statement and policy is discussed in turn, for that way you will discover and better understand your managers and how they see their work in your organisation.

Note: All 'NOT SURE' responses score 0.

(1) NO: Screening interviews are the the responsibility of the personnel department or the senior person from the area where the potential employee is going to work. Your management time is valuable and should only be used to confirm the final choice.

(2) NO: If you are going to be an effective manager you should avoid situations which undermine the position of one of your team. You should only undertake such a visit at the request of one of your team members, not at the request of another manager.

(3) YES: Recurring problems for which there are existing satisfactory answers can be dealt with swiftly by anyone who knows the answer. There is no harm in you, the manager, advising a new member of your team about an existing solution. It shows interest and consideration.

(4) NO: Telling people what you would do without finding out how they intend to tackle the problem undermines their initiative. It also reduces the probability of better solutions being put forward. This approach will eventually lead to you the manager making all the decisions—both good and bad.

(5) NO: Interfering with the communication channels that are more relevant to the members of your team is bad management. Give the team member the information and let them deal with it. Once you have delegated a task only intervene if requested to do so.

(6) YES: Bonuses related to performance should always be used to reinforce a team member's motivation. Money is a great motivator but the relationship between the money and the performance must be clearly established. That is part of your job.

(7) YES OR NO IS OK: Although this is not managing it is an activity that comes with the job. Managers are the organisations' representatives in the community.

(8) NO: Tell your ideas to someone who can turn them into a plan or layout. Do not indulge yourself with this type of exercise; you are a manager not a draughtsman.

(9) YES: Discussing with your team how your ideas might affect them, and then listening to and answering their questions, is part of your job as a manager. This method avoids the 'fear of the unknown' syndrome. Mushroom management techniques (keeping everyone in the dark and pouring manure on them occasionally) has no place in an effective organisation.

Is it Managing?   DEVELOPMENT GUIDE 1

(10) YES: A manager is responsible for seeing that the team achieves its objectives. Each member of your team will have a responsibility to the team as a whole. If any member of your team fails to perform, ultimately the whole team will suffer. In such instances your job, as the manager, is:

(a) To ensure that the team continues towards the achievement of its objectives. (This means making sure that the urgent task is completed without further delay.)

(b) To find out why your team member was unable to tackle the task agreed. Helping a team member overcome a performance problem is also an essential management task.

(11) YES: You hurt people when you introduce changes into their lives without consulting them. Such actions suggest to people that you don't care and that they are unimportant. If you want changes to work make sure that the people that can make them work are on your side. That means fully explaining the changes and modifying them if necessary.

(12) NO: Let the relevant technical team member go. Technical developments will probably affect them more than they will you. They are also more likely to ask the right questions and will be able to give you a better idea of the implications.

(13) YES: A good manager always has a good working relationship with his immediate boss. Arranging to discuss progress with him on a regular basis (once a week) is managerial, even if occasionally it's only on the phone.

(14) NO: Give this job to one of your team. It will show them how much you trust them.

(15) YES: If your key team members are able to discuss with you the possible effects of these proposed expenditure items they are likely to be more realistic. This is common sense management.

(16) NO: Although most organisations require their managers to fill in forms and authorise cheques, it is not managerial work, it is status work which reinforces the 'them and us' syndrome. Effective managers delegate many of these routine responsibilities when and wherever possible.

(17) NO: You should try to get one of your team to do most of this type of work. By all means sign routine forms and cheques but don't, if you can avoid it, fill them out. That should be the job of your secretary.

(18) YES: A good manager must understand and have confidence in the budget he or she is responsible for.

(19) YES: People only grow and develop if they receive feedback; that's what review procedures are all about. Unfortunately some managers find them very difficult. Reviewing the performance of your team members can be achieved in a number of ways. As long as it is done regularly (once a month) and is positive and constructive then the method used is not too critical. Later in the book I will provide details of a straightforward and successful method.

(20) YES: Although this would be a highly controversial policy in any organisation. A disciplined and accurate approach is needed for an organisation's budgeting process otherwise the whole exercise will be a waste of time. Limiting alterations in this way will ensure that managers take the budget process seriously. Variance will occur of course and the guilty parties will be easy to identify.

THE 'HANDS ON' MANAGER'S JOB

Now that you have had a chance to discuss with your managers some of the basics, it's time for you both to start examining jobs more closely.

Before we move on to the next discovery exercise I would like you and your management team to consider what I call the core 'hands on' management activities. I have given each of these a catch name which I hope encapsulates the task involved. If you have the facilities, you might like to prepare overhead transparencies using these catch names to support your presentation and discussions. The activities are as follows:

(1) *TOP-TEAM SUPPORTER* *ASSISTING SENIOR MANAGEMENT RE BUDGETS, TARGETS AND THE ACHIEVEMENT OF OBJECTIVES.*

Really effective managers are not passive bystanders in the organisation planning process. They like to prepare, with their team, the budget for their own area of responsibility. They expect their team members to know 'how many beans make five' and it is very unlikely that they will accept that 'the accounts department knows best'. They usually develop a broad outline of targets for their area of responsibility and then conduct discussions with their team on the details. Their team members know that they can criticise and change things as long as they have prepared their arguments in a professional and positive way. Likewise really effective managers will never be frightened to tackle board level management about organisation objectives and will expect to be invited to contribute to the decisions that decide them. This is because, above everything else, success in the role of top team supporter is based on a sharp awareness of what is going on and what is most likely to happen in the future.

(2) *OWN-TEAM COACH* *MOTIVATING, MOULDING AND MONITORING THE PERFORMANCE OF EACH MEMBER OF THEIR TEAM.*

To manage successfully it is necessary to know a lot about human behaviour, and to be alive to the fact that good human relations in the workplace makes the difference. All the members of an effective manager's team will know what is expected of them and how their performance is being measured. Effective managers will, in turn, know the strengths and weaknesses of each team member and will seek to coach each of them to their full potential. They also know that feedback is the key in the coaching process; a job well done is always rewarded and mistakes are always turned into positive learning experiences. People will always want to work for a manager who lets them know where they are, where they are going and, most of all, lets them have a say in both.

(3) *JACKETS-OFF COMRADE* *ASSISTING MEMBERS OF THEIR TEAM WITH JOB SPECIFIC PROBLEMS.*

Effective managers know all about the work their people have to do and trust them to do it. They never take over in a problem situation, unless invited, and always give the team every opportunity to find their own solution. Other managers cannot pressure them into undermining their team by asking them to intervene in problem situations. They are always ready to help when asked to do so and never use status to impress. When the need arises they can be relied upon to take off their jackets and work alongside the rest of the team.

(4) *BUCK STOPS CAPTAIN* *ORGANISING, ALLOCATING AND CONTROLLING THE WORK REQUIRED OF THEIR TEAM.*

A manager accepts responsibility for the work the team does and is required to do.

Effective managers usually distribute work on a broad allocation basis and allow the team to agree the details among themselves. They use both ability and development as criteria when allocating key tasks and control progress by using 'exception' management. They plan ahead as far as possible and maintain an overview of all the work for which the team is responsible. The team experiences few unpleasant surprises but when problems do occur they do know where the buck stops.

(5) *WAVING THE FLAG CHEER-LEADER* *REPRESENTING THEIR AREA OF RESPONSIBILITY ON BEHALF OF THE ORGANISATION.*

It is the responsibility of all managers generally to represent the area of the organisation for which they are responsible, both internally and externally. Effective managers try hard to limit the amount of time spent on such activities and are not afraid to delegate these tasks to key team members. They regard such delegation as being good for team member development. When attending meetings they try to act as the team's representative and seek to find the right balance between team and organisational needs. At all times they try to keep the team well informed on organisational matters which affect them.

CLASSIFYING MANAGEMENT TASKS

The core activities and how the 'hands on' manager might respond to them were provided to stimulate your managers into thinking about how they manage. Your managers can now classify their own work under the same or similar common activity area headings. The five areas are repeated here for your convenience.

(1) Assisting senior management re budgets, targets and the achievement of objectives.

(2) Motivating, moulding and monitoring the performance of each member of their team.

(3) Assisting members of their team with job specific problems.

(4) Organising, allocating and controlling the work required of their team.

(5) Representing their area of responsibility on behalf of the organisation.

At this stage a word of warning: most managers find this very difficult to do. You will get lots of excuses and statements like:

'My work is unique.'

'It's hard to quantify my work in this way.'

'I can't see the relevance of these headings to my job.'

You have to win this battle if you are going to remove the mystery of how people manage in your organisation. One way forward is to use the manager's preference for oral rather than written communication. Start the process in a group setting using an adapted brainstorming technique. Put up descriptions on a board and allow the 'knock on' effect to work for you; you will soon have a good number of activities to classify.

You might also like to reproduce, as a handout, the list of statements made by managers about their work illustrated in Development Guide 2. Ask your managers to classify them under the headings as a practice exercise.

It is important, at this point, that you really encourage your managers to think about the reality of their jobs and to discuss with each other how they operate. Ensure that no criticism is levelled at any single manager. It is necessary for you to be very positive to get the co-operation this exercise needs. Since the core activities will represent only a part of their work, get them to list all the other things they do under headings they make up for themselves.

DISCOVERY EXERCISE

Brainstorming/classification exercise using Development Guide 2.   *Allow 60 minutes.*

Managers classifying their own work under the five core activity headings.   *Allow 90 minutes.*

Classifying Management Activities

DEVELOPMENT GUIDE 2

NAME: _____   DATE: _____

TASK You should read each of the activity descriptions listed 1 to 9 and match each of them to one of the five common activity areas. Put the number you select from 1 to 5 under the activity area column. The answers can be found in the appendix (see page 169).

General description	Activity area
(1) 'I have to carry out the 1 month and 12 month sales forecasts for my department and account for all the past variances.'	
(2) 'Each month the sales office provide me with a rolling forecast of what they want. It's normally one month firm and two months flexible.'	
(3) 'On average I attend ten meetings a month two of which are at head office and one of which is with our main supplier.'	
(4) 'I have thirty staff two of whom act as my deputies. Our work is seasonal and revolves around the annual budget and accounts. I split the department down into costing and financial matters and allocate the work accordingly. It seems to work.'	
(5) 'Part of my job is training. Each month we hold a team meeting at which two of the team are required to role-play customer situations. I provide the guidance and everyone learns something including me.	
(6) 'I seem to spend half of my day on the phone chasing up missing parts for my engineers and the other half planning the work load for next week. It never goes smoothly here. The person who shouts loudest always gets priority.'	
(7) 'I like to walk through the works at least once a day; people bring me their problems and I am able to prevent things getting out of hand. It also gets me out of the office.'	
(8) 'My main duty is to manage the administrative assistants for the social workers in the field. I have drawn up a support rota and call regular meetings between the two groups. Before I came nobody even talked about co-operation if they could avoid it. It works better now.'	
(9) When I arrived the existing staff were demoralised and staff turnover was a major problem. I couldn't pay them any more so I tried to make their working day more interesting. I plan with each member of staff their work schedule for the week and try to stick to it. Nobody has left for the last four months.'	

THE IMPORTANCE OF 'HANDS ON' TIME

After your managers have completed all the job classification tasks give them a rest and let the results sink in. They are now seriously thinking about what they do and the processes of self-analysis are starting to work. You may find that certain managers want to change the way they do things. They may increase the amount of work they delegate. Watch to see if they are starting to treat their people differently; you may be surprised. All these things are encouraging signs that they are starting to become more 'hands on'.

The next stage is probably the most difficult in the book to complete. It can be tedious but the results in improved performance are always very dramatic. You are going to ask your managers to record how they spend their time at work. Yes, every minute!

David Marples of Trinity College, Cambridge, once said: 'Managers have three resources at their disposal; their own skill and experience; the goodwill and trust of their colleagues; and time.'

Managers tend to work under a lot of pressure. In many instances this is self-generated, the result of not having created enough time to do the important things properly. This is not surprising since very few managers are prepared for the job of managing before they have to do it. They often find themselves caught up in a whirlwind of demands for their attention with no idea of the best course of action.

Although I am a great advocate of learning while doing, the process has to be structured for it to be successful. Managers have to make important decisions every day; they need time to think about those decisions and training to help make them. Because managers should be concerned about the future as well as the immediate present they also need time to think forward; managers can only be pro-active if they create the time necessary to be so. By getting your managers to examine how they use their time you are likely to avoid a number of costly problems. Here are some examples.

(1) *The 'hanging onto the old job'* **problem** Many managers like to continue to be involved with the job they were doing before they became a manager. After all that was a job they were really good at wasn't it? They try to impose the way they did the job on the new job holder and spend a lot of valuable management time trying to do someone else's job. Before you can say 'hands on' you find you have lost a good specialist and gained a poor manager.

(2) *The 'progress has been delayed until after I've dealt with this'* **problem** Some managers find the pressure of managing becomes so great that the only movement they are able to generate is from one crisis to another. They are so busy dealing with every little detail that they have

forgotten to allow time to create tomorrow's objectives. You end up with a manager so busy putting out fires that he's stopped looking for the man with the box of matches.

(3) *The 'system doesn't allow for that'* **problem** Some managers get railroaded into continuing outdated systems because they don't have enough time to evaluate them. In trying to make this work they find themselves being run by the system rather than deciding which system they should be running. In the meantime your organisation just gets more and more out of date.

(4) *The 'I'll do that this evening'* **problem** Managers who take work home just to keep their heads above water have lost the battle. Before long they find themselves with more new problems than the old ones they were trying to solve. A balanced life style is a prerequisite to successful management. 'Hands on' managers enjoy a life outside work; this enables them to be more objective in decision-making and provides the energy that they need to win during the day. If you have managers who have to take work home on a regular basis then either they can't manage or you are asking them to manage too much.

(5) *The 'leave that to me'* **problem** Lack of a willingness to delegate is the downfall of many a manager. Of course all managers think they can do the job of each of their team better than the team member. What they can't do is all of the jobs at once better than the team. It is essential that they find the time to do the things they must do as managers and delegate the rest.

CREATING MORE 'HANDS ON' TIME

To start the process of creating more time for managing, you will need something to arouse the interest of your managers. The easiest solution is to show them a video/film on time management. There must be at least 15 different videos on time management on the market and most of them have supporting exercises built around them. I strongly recommend *Time to Think* which is distributed by Rank. This video really puts across a manager's need to create time for managing. Review the film a couple of times yourself and try to list the key points it raises. After you have shown the film ask your managers to write down on a piece of paper what percentages of their work time they spend on the core activities they have just identified. When they have done that get them to break the times down again into very specific work activities such as the following:

- Letter-writing.
- Telephoning.
- Talking to other managers.

- Talking with their boss.
- Dealing with problems from members of their team.
- Socialising.
- Lunch breaks.
- Improving their knowledge.

Ten minutes is normally long enough for the first task and 15 minutes is about right for the second.

If you really want to catch them out ask them this question before you show them the video film! When they have completed these exercises tell them that you want them to copy the example of the manager featured in the video film. By prepared to show the film again if necessary.

DISCOVERY EXERCISE

Estimating the time spent on the core management activities.

Allow 10 minutes.

Breaking down the time spent on specific work tasks

Allow 15 minutes.

Now we come to the tough part: getting your managers to keep an activity diary. The instructions for completing the activity diary are presented as Development Guide 3. How long the activity diary should be kept for is a matter for agreement between you and your managers. There are several ways it can be done.

(1) Every day for a week or month.

(2) One different day each week until you have a representative week or month.

(3) In detail for a week and then in outline for a month to ensure that the detailed week is representative.

The form for keeping an activity diary is provided as Development Guide 4. Feel free to modify it to suit your own organisation's needs.

Also provided for reproduction and distribution is Development Guide 5, which is displayed on pages 16, 17 and 18. This is an example of a manager's completed activity diary for one day. Development Guide 6 provides a set of charts which represent a comparative analysis of actual time against estimated time and a report on what was gained from the experience by the same manager. You do not have to follow these examples to the letter: let your managers have as much freedom as they need to express themselves about their use of time and to tell you about what they have learnt from the exercise.

DISCOVERY EXERCISE

Keeping an activity diary.

Keeping a Management Activity Diary

DEVELOPMENT GUIDE 3

OBJECTIVE The objective of this exercise is to collect information on how you spend your time. It is important that the information is collected in a uniform manner as it will be collated for analysis at the end of the exercise.

METHOD You can record each activity yourself or get one of your team to observe you and record what you are doing. As long as the recording method is consistent you may interchange who does the recording as often as you like.

Normally your working day comprises various activities; some last a long time while others, if you are a typical manager, only last a few minutes. You should try and record all the activities both long and short.

Development Guide 4 has been provided as a guide to how you could lay out the information. You do not have to stick to that design but you should have columns which cover the following:

(A) THE TIME OF THE ACTIVITY The time of day when each activity occurred should be recorded as accurately as possible.

(B) THE DURATION OF THE ACTIVITY The time each activity takes should be recorded. Activities of less than three minutes should be recorded only if they are regarded as important. If in doubt record it.

(C) THE SEQUENCE OF THE ACTIVITY It is helpful for future consideration of the activity to be able to identify the sequence in which it occurred. If the last activity on day one is 12 then the first activity on day two is 13 and so on.

(D) THE EVENTS RELATED TO THE ACTIVITY Try to record the events as precisely as possible. You personally spoke to or spoke with . . . ; telephone calls made to and received from . . . ; meetings with and for what purpose . . . ; visits by and to . . . ; etc.

(E) THE CONTACTS THAT OCCURRED DURING THE ACTIVITY Where possible provide names or initials. If you use initials make sure that you have some form of indexing system that enables you to identify the people concerned by their initials.

(F) THE ADDITIONAL INFORMATION NEEDED TO DEFINE THE ATMOSPHERE SURROUNDING THE ACTIVITY Were voices raised? Was it a crisis? Could it have been handled another way?

When you have completed the exercise try to arrive at the percentage of time allocated to the major activities, i.e. time spent at meetings, on the telephone, with members of your team, with your boss, clients, etc.
Good luck.

DEVELOPMENT GUIDE 4

ACTIVITY DIARY

DATE FROM	DATE TO	NAME	JOB TITLE	
		COMPANY		PAGE NO

TIME	DURATION	SEQUENT NUMBER	ACTIVITY	CONTACTS	ADDITIONAL INFORMATION

Do NOT use a page for more than one day. 'Subsequent Number' will follow on from previous page. 'Date From' and 'To' will show time Diary kept. Use dashes at edges to draw horizontal lines if needed. Show 'Duration' in minutes

MERCURY

SIGNATURE _____

ACTIVITY DIARY

NAME		JOB TITLE	
DATE FROM Tues 23rd October	DATE TO	COMPANY	PAGE NO 4/17

TIME	DURATION	SEQUENT NUMBER	ACTIVITY	CONTACTS	ADDITIONAL INFORMATION
9.00	30	23	Discuss visit to Kings Lynn to see new IBM installation. Assess what was learnt and relevance to us	AHD	We are looking at replacement of current computer. These activities are taking up far more time than normal at present Although day to day running is not my responsibility there are so many problems have been asked to try to solve by AHD
9.30	10	24	Programmer having problems with getting time for a particular test job	CP	
9.40	10	25	Request from user for out of hours running time for a special job. Got details, arranged times	TN RC	
9.50	40	24	Discuss problem of test job and other complaints received on similar lines. Arrange meeting for 2.00 pm to get all facts	AHD	RC Operations Supervisor
10.30	3	26	Phone call from previous employee for reference		
10.33	8	27	User calls to ask whether his requested changes will be on time, checked that they would and reassured him	AD	
10.41	5	28	Open, read and throw away mail	GN GWE	GWE Systems Analyst Programmer
10.46	9	29	Talk to chief operator about YOP employee reading book when there was work to do	RC CR	CR Does not really seem that interested in doing anything but finishing his course with minimum effort.
10.55	10	26	Gather information & dictate letter for reference		
11.05	5	30	Loo		

MERCURY

SIGNATURE _____

Do NOT use a page for more than one day. 'Subsequent Number' will follow on from previous page. 'Date From' and 'To' will show time Diary kept. Use dashes at edges to draw horizontal lines if needed. Show 'Duration' in minutes

ACTIVITY DIARY

NAME		JOB TITLE
	COMPANY	

DATE FROM	DATE TO	PAGE NO
Tues 23rd October		5/17

TIME	DURATION	SEQUENT NUMBER	ACTIVITY	CONTACTS	ADDITIONAL INFORMATION
11.10	41	31	User has problem with program apparently giving wrong results; seems OK when details explained	AC	AC Head of Management Services. I tend to deal with this guy as there is often no problem at all
11.51	7	26	Finish off reference for ex-employee		
11.58	42	32	Incorrect figures appearing on screens. This program has not been changed so no real reason for errors	AHD	
12.40	2	33	Read circular on printer silencers and pass on to possibly interested users	TN RC	I seem to read anything that lands on my desk immediately
12.42	53	34	Lunch		
13.35	15	32	Continue with incorrect figures on screen Decide that it is a file with incorrect data having been placed on it		This became an item on the agenda of meeting below
13.50	13	35	Electricity consumption figures		
14.03	7	36	Report that users are giving each other their passwords, get passwords changed and users informed not to do it		I am reading things on my desk as soon as they arrive again
14.10	46	24	Meeting with AHD to discuss problems about operations section and how to solve	AHD	
14.56	25	37	Phone GN to obtain information concerning errors in Bonus System. Phone RC to get the same	GN RC	

Do NOT use a page for more than one day. 'Subsequent Number' will follow on from previous page. 'Date From' and 'To' will show time Diary kept. Use dashes at edges to draw horizontal lines if needed. Show 'Duration' in minutes

SIGNATURE _____

MERCURY

DEVELOPMENT GUIDE 3

ACTIVITY DIARY

DATE FROM Tues 23rd October	DATE TO	NAME
		COMPANY

NAME JOB TITLE

PAGE NO 6/17

TIME	DURATION	SEQUENT NUMBER	ACTIVITY	CONTACTS	ADDITIONAL INFORMATION
15.21	2	38	Phone call with query on waiting list transferred to GWE	GWE	
15.23	17	37	Continue analysing bonus error		
15.40	1	39	Phone wrong number		
15.41	19	37	Discover cause of bonus error, explain to Operations what caused it to ensure that it does not happen again	RC CJ JM	CJ is Computer Operator
16.00	39	40	Schedule some work for housing repairs system		
16.39	10	41	Filing		
16.49	41	24	Continue with problems on operations section and try to look at all the problems		I suppose I should be getting someone else to do this
17.30		42	Home		
19.35	5	43	Phone call to say that repairs systems has gone wrong. I am first person to be in. Say will go in later	CJ	We have a call-in late list so that the same person does not get called in all the time
21.15	225	43	Sort out the problem and rerun program		

MERCURY

SIGNATURE

DEVELOPMENT GUIDE 6

Activity diary analysis 1: Time spent

Activity	Estimated time usage %	Actual time usage %
Thinking	7	4.5
Planning	10	3.5
Work assignments	12	5.5
Progress reporting	12	5.5
Staff interviews	4	2.5
Telephone	4	1.5
Meetings with outside organisations	9	7.0
Meetings with other depts.	8	10.0
Problem-solving	10	38.5
Meetings with superior	8	8.5
Reading reports	7	0.5
Writing reports	5	5.5
Reading trade magazines	1	0.0
Dealing with salesmen	1	1.0
Honeywell users assoc.	1	0.0
Eating, etc.	1	0.5
Routine paperwork	0	4.5
Dealing with mail	0	1.0

Activity diary analysis 2: priorities ranked according to time estimated as allocated and actually spent

Estimated	Actual
1 Work assignments	1 Problem-solving
2 Progress reporting	2 Meetings with other depts.
3 Staff interviews	3 Meetings with superior
4 Meetings with other depts.	4 Meetings with outside orgs.
5 Problem-solving	5 Work assignments
	6 Progress reporting
	7 Writing reports

DEVELOPMENT GUIDE 6

Activity diary analysis 3: Estimates versus actual spent time on individual activities

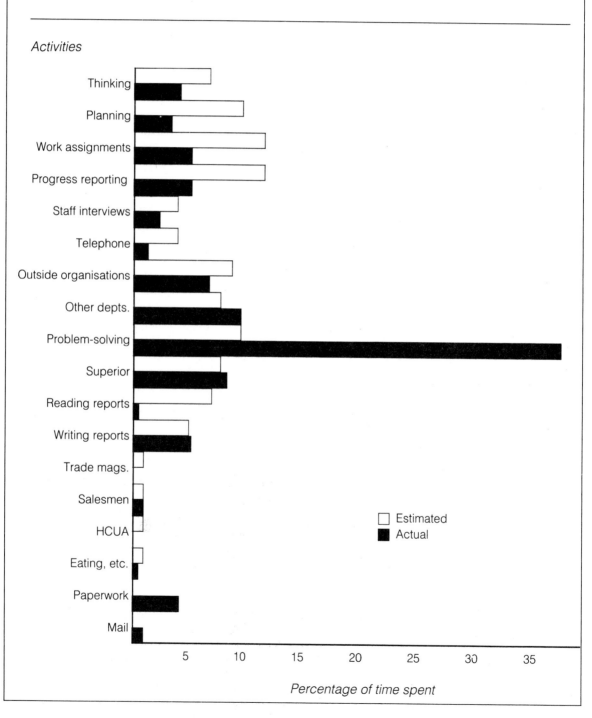

Activities

Percentage of time spent

DEVELOPMENT GUIDE 6

Activity diary analysis 3: Comments

(1) Problem-solving was much higher than estimated, taking up to neary 40% of time. It would be nice to say that this was unusually high but I think that may not be true.

(2) Work assignments, progress reporting and staff interviews took much less time than originally estimated. This is worrying as it means that I am over estimating the amount of time spent controlling and making sure they are working properly.

(3) Time spent thinking was lower than originally estimated, perhaps indicating that I am not thinking things through as thoroughly as I estimated.

(4) Time spent in meetings with other departments, meetings with outside organisations, superior and writing reports was estimated almost correctly.

(5) Report reading was virtually nil (0.5%) as opposed to 7% estimated.

(6) I did not allow any time for various paperwork functions (photocopying, filing etc.) whereas they took 4.5% of my time. Perhaps I should not be doing those at all.

(7) The telephone rang much less frequently (1.5%) than I estimated (4%).

(8) I noticed that on many occasions I was dealing with information as it hit my desk, rather than scheduling it. I should spend more time planning and scheduling my time rather than just doing things when they arrive. This will cause fewer breaks in my day.

(9) Many times I had to stop doing something to deal with a personal caller or other interruption. I need to make appointments so that I can avoid my time becoming too fragmented.

Activity diary analysis 4: Conclusions

I was very disturbed at the small amount of time I spent planning and controlling my staff. I seemed to spend most of my time fire-fighting rather than solving problems, planning and getting feedback. It would be nice to think that this week was exceptional in the number of problems encountered. However, to be strictly honest I do not believe that it was.

At some points during the week I attempted proper problem-solving rather than fire-fighting; much of this effort was wasted, however, because of constant interruptions. To be fair, most of these interruptions could have been avoided by the proper use of appointments and schedules.

I must ensure than I adopt the following procedures:

(1) Plan and schedule my day.

(2) Allow and keep to times for staff problem-solving, work assignments, progress reports etc.

(3) Fix appointments and stick to them more.

(4) Do not solve problems as they hit my desk; fit them into the schedule taking urgency into account.

(5) Try to ensure that problems are solved rather than patched up.

CHAPTER SUMMARY

You have now completed the first, and in many ways the most difficult, chapter so let's check progress.

(1) Your managers now know why they are and will continue to be necessary.

(2) Your managers now know what effective managers should do.

(3) Your managers now know the importance of creating time for managing.

This knowledge should lead to action on the part of your managers; they should be:

(1) Looking at their own work with a very critical eye.

(2) Modifying their work patterns so that they become more managerial, more 'hands on'.

(3) Trying to improve the amount of time they have for management activities, creating more management thinking time.

If these things are happening then you have established the foundation for effective management in your organisation and are ready for the next chapter.

2

ASSESSING MANAGERIAL SKILLS

If managerial effectiveness is to be improved managers must first understand which of their characteristics and skills need developing. This chapter considers what the attributes of the 'ideal manager' might be; the skills required for effective managerial performance and ways of acquiring them.

Your managers will be recommended to take a number of personality and aptitude assessments, two of which are included in the chapter. The results of these assessments can then be matched with the characteristics and skills that you and they jointly agreed are needed for effectiveness in each of their jobs. By taking your managers through this process you will be able to help them consider ways of capitalising on their individual strengths and reducing their weaknesses.

A word of warning: personality and aptitude assessment is always a sensitive issue. The processes in this chapter require a co-operative and positive attitude from all the parties involved; take your time and modify or reduce the assessment process if you feel it is starting to have a negative effect: if you handle the process with care the results will be most rewarding.

At the end of this chapter both you and each member of your management team will have a complete understanding of their personal managerial profile. You will have learned a lot about what makes each of your managers tick and will have achieved the following objective in your quest to create the 'hands on' management team.

▶ *The identification of the characteristics and skills needed for effective performance in each manager's job.*

THE BASIS FOR THE 'IDEAL MANAGER'

What characteristics make up the ideal manager? To some extent the answer depends on what has to be managed. Managing a hotel is not the same as managing a container terminal or a football team or a recruitment agency or a hospital. Each enterprise and its components has unique features which managers must understand before they can manage any of the components effectively. However, allowing for a period of time to adjust to job specific requirements, a good manager should be able to manage anything. Professor Reg Revans proved this when he swopped the manager of a UK oil refinery with the manager of a Belgian bank. To be an effective manager, then, is not just being very good at the business of the organisation: the best football players rarely become the best football managers and the best nurses rarely become the best hospital administrators. Remember:

Managing the work is fundamentally different from doing the work.

This doesn't mean that hospital administrators do not need to know what a nurse does or the circumstances under which a nurse's tasks are carried out. In my experience the best managers can, if asked, always describe the features and problems of the tasks of those they manage. Once managers no longer understand the nature of the work of their team members, then the problems really start. In fact most manager/worker conflicts are the result of the lack of this kind of knowledge on the part of the manager. Effective management requires a manager to possess job specific skills as well as managing skills.

THE SKILLS AND THE JOB OF MANAGING

Now we come to the crunch. The skills of managing are, in my opinion, embedded in personality and aptitude; remember:

Some people have the right characteristics and aptitudes that will enable them to become effective managers while others do not.

Unfortunately management is one of the few professions which does not accept this truism. Just consider some of the reasons commonly given for the appointment of managers:

- Managers make other people managers because they are good at their existing job and want to reward them.
- Managers make other people managers because they have the specialist knowledge or skills they think are needed for a project.
- Managers make other people managers because they have MBAs or PhDs in management-related theories.
- Managers make other people managers because they have similar characteristics to themselves.
- Managers make other people managers who won't pose a threat to their own authority and position.

- Managers make other people managers because its the only way they can give them the money they need to keep them.

I would estimate that less than 25% of managers are appointed because they have proved themselves to be effective in managerial situations. This is a very worrying state of affairs.

What then are the skills of managing? I identify five skills:

(1) PERCEPTUAL SKILLS *The ability to sense that the normal events occurring in and around the organisation could, in certain circumstances, present problems or opportunities which require managerial action.*

'Hands on' managers will normally be able to see things earlier than everyone else; this enables them to be pro-active on the majority of problems and opportunities they encounter.

(2) ANALYTICAL SKILLS *The ability to determine the significant components of a system, process method, set of ideas or body of information when these are presented for managerial action.*

To be effective managers must be able to separate causes from symptoms. 'Hands on' managers will be able to look at a group of objects and decide which are significant and which are not in any given situations. This enables them to make more effective managerial decisions.

(3) CREATIVE SKILLS *The ability to overcome fixations which normally constrain the range of possible solutions seen for a given problem or normally inhibit the exploitation of opportunities.*

The ability to be able to use both sides of the brain, the logical and the creative, is an important managerial attribute; it enables the manager to think up new ways of doing things when the old ways no longer prove adequate. Organisations, as a result of structure and policy, limit creative actions; managers with creative skills are therefore necessary to stop the organisation ossifying. 'Hands on' managers can always 'break the mould'.

(4) JUDICIAL OR JUDGEMENTAL SKILLS *The ability to use both deductive and inductive reasoning in reaching decisions and solving problems when presented with multifarious information about situations requiring management action.*

'Hands on' managers like making decisions and can handle the pressures that always seem to accompany the managerial decision-making process. They can make decisions from narrow and specific evidence or very broad and general information. They are capable of handling the ambiguous data coming at them from all directions and making sense of it. They will have a good track record of being right and usually make the correct moves in situations of great sensitivity, such as negotiations.

(5) *INTER-PERSONAL SKILLS* *The ability to initiate interactions with and between people which successfully achieve organisation objectives.*

The skills which can be groupcd under this heading are the most important in management. Managers with real management jobs have to deal with people more than they have to deal with anything else. This part of the manager's job can be summarised as:

Getting the team to work.
Getting the team to work with each other.
Getting the team to work with other teams.

Negotiations, interviews, the delegation of work, staff discipline, morale and motivation will involve the use of inter-personal skills. A manager cannot be effective without first class inter-personal skills.

Most managerial activities require a mix of the skills, the weight of each skill required for any one managerial task differing with the task.

We should now consider the development and improvement of these characteristics and skills.

PERSONALITY AND THE JOB OF MANAGING

Now you know what skills you want your managers to possess let's retrace our steps a little and reconsider the 'ideal manager' concept. I want you to write down what personality characteristics you would expect to see a skilled manager display. You should try to use the skill definitions I have provided as a reference, but if you have strong views of your own as to what constitutes managerial skill then use them. This is an important task so take at least 15 minutes to complete it.

DISCOVERY EXERCISE

Listing the personality characteristics of a skilled manager.   *Allow 15 minutes.*

Let me guess at some of the answers you might have written.
(1) *Confident with* lots of *self-belief.*
(2) *Stimulating* and *participative* with an ability to motivate people and get the best out of them.

(3) *Intelligent* and *quick-witted* with a liking for decision-making and problem-solving.

(4) *Assertive* and *tough-minded* with lots of energy and drive.

(5) *Competitive* with a need to win.

(6) *Innovative* with a desire to *create* as well as perpetuate.

(7) *Intuitive* as well as *analytical* in decision-making situations.

We have a rough idea of the skills and characteristics we would like our managers to possess but we need to find out those that they actually do possess.

MEASURING MANAGERIAL CHARACTERISTICS AND SKILLS

Measuring a manager's potential ability to act in a skilled way is unfortunately not straightforward. It is of course possible to set tasks requiring the use of the appropriate skills to see how your managers handle them. This is fine as a developmental exercise but is unlikely to be reliable as a true measure of performance, especially in a one-off simulation situation. The method I have found very reliable and have used for the last nine years is personality and aptitude assessment. It requires a degree of subjective judgement on your part plus a frank discussion about the results. This said, this type of assessment does get quickly to the core of the manager and reveals the significant strengths and weaknesses better than any other method I know.

The first thing to be said about personality and aptitude assessment is that it is just another formalised way of assessing people. Like a driving test, an examination or an interview, these assessments are designed to give us more information about the person, they are not a replacement for our judgement and good sense. What they do is provide us with a lot of information quickly.

We assess or judge people informally almost constantly: it is a human trait that we all practise everyday. We need to make sense of the people and things around us and we measure them against references we store in our brain. For example, we all have perceptions about people who drive motor-bikes, like animals, bet on horses, do crossword puzzles, wear bowler hats, etc., and we expect them to act in a certain way in given situations. We also place them in situations where we expect them to feel at home. Bowler hats in the City, gamblers in the betting shop or at the races etc.

If you know that a manager tends to behave in a certain way you can place him or her in a situation which needs management and anticipate the results. You won't always be right, because people are full of surprises, but you will tend to do it regardless. Personality and aptitude assessments will help you reduce the surprise element in this process by giving you a better picture of each manager's behavioural tendencies.

Once you have that knowledge you will be able to associate the behaviour with the potential for skilled performance.

Personality assessments range from those that are no better than fortune telling to those that are backed up by years of detailed academic research. The first assessment I suggest you try is one written by myself. It is the 'Watts-Manager's Approach to Creativity Indicator'—'MAC' for short.

WHAT MAC IS ALL ABOUT

MAC has been specifically designed to enable you and your managers to gain a greater understanding of their approach to the management skill of creativity; that is, creativity as applied mainly to problem-solving and opportunity exploitation. Three personality traits are measured by MAC. They are: innovative disposition, occupational pre-occupation and organisational compliance.

(1) *INNOVATIVE DISPOSITION* The desire to think up new ways of solving problems and exploiting situations; the ability to develop and accept from staff solutions which transcend the organisational constraints surrounding a problem situation; the need for tasks which seem to benefit from a radical approach to problem solving and decision making; an inclination to allow staff a high degree of freedom in the way they work and tackle tasks; and, in general, a preference for being able to adopt a free-rein approach to problem situations and a dislike of overt guidance and rules related to allocated tasks.

(2) *OCCUPATIONAL PREOCCUPATION* The need to double check work and ensure that every detail has been attended to; the ability to be able to follow precisely a plan or procedure; the need to be given all the evidence before taking any action; the inclination to give very precise instructions with all delegated tasks; an expectation that staff will follow guidelines very closely and the tendency to check to ensure the 'detail' has been attended to; and, in general, a preference for being able to adopt a systematic and methodical approach to problem solving with a dislike of risk situations.

(3) *ORGANISATIONAL COMPLIANCE* The desire to ensure that the organisation's policies are followed when solving problems and making decisions; the ability to make solutions 'fit' the organisation's norms and rules; the need to ensure that the organisation is not adversely affected by the solutions to problems generated by staff; a willingness, in most instances, to allow staff to solve problems as they wish as long as they observe and respect the organisation's rules and policies; and, in general, working towards what is 'best' for the organisation in preference to what might be considered 'best' in any one particular problem situation.

You can see that we have moved away from guess-work and simple behaviour/action predictions into a much more precise behaviour/action measurement mode.

Let's now take things a little further. I would like you to look at the Development Guide 7. Reproduced are two sets of statements made by managers, 'O' MANAGERS AND 'UO' MANAGERS; do not worry about what 'O' and 'UO' means at this stage—just read the test for the two managers. Take about five minutes for this task.

DISCOVERY EXERCISE

Reading the text for O and UO managers.   *Allow 5 minutes.*

Now I want you to decide which of the two management statements you would be most likely to make. Yes, I know you would like to use the best sentences from each set of statements but that's not possible. All behavioural tendencies have both positive and negative characteristics, so choose. If you want to, at this stage, you can also ask your managers to do the same thing. When you have made your choice put the information to one side because you are now ready to take MAC, which is reproduced as Development Guide 8.

I recommend that you complete the MAC assessment before tackling it with your managers; this will give you more confidence in handling their questions when they get their results.

DISCOVERY EXERCISE

Do MAC.   *Allow 15 minutes maximum.*

Although MAC has been laid out for you to reproduce, you may prefer the convenience of purpose-designed copies. These can be obtained via the follow-up service detailed in the appendix. Through this service you will be able to purchase sets of MAC questions complete with a computer program. The program will run on any IBM compatible computer that will accept MS-DOS 2.11, and will generate individual reports, create a database of results and analyse the collected data. This service is available to all qualified management developers.

When you have completed and marked your MAC assessment you can find out what your scores mean by turning to the appendix.

MAC
The characteristics of 'O' and 'UO' managers

DEVELOPMENT GUIDE 7

The 'O' Manager

As a manager I consider it is essential that I be regarded by my seniors, peers and staff as efficient. To achieve efficiency requires discipline and precision, and I take great care to ensure that what I do and say is accurate and based on established and proven methods and procedures. In my opinion too many errors in organisations come from lack of attention to detail. I regard my ability to maintain a high degree of accuracy, over a long period of time, even when tackling detailed work, as one of my main strengths.

I think it is important for those I work with to know how I will react to their actions, so I try to ensure that my reactions and general behaviour remain consistent. I also think continuity is needed for the well-being of the organisation and try to avoid radical changes in work patterns and methods. I find most new problems can be solved by modifying or refining existing solutions and approaches. In general, I prefer evolution to revolution as a way of making progress. In my opinion too many managers adopt change just for change's sake.

Some people regard me as over-cautious and have suggested that I am too compliant and conformist. My answer to such comments is that rules are essential for the proper conduct of organisational life. New approaches and methods will have to be well tested before they are acceptable to me.

If I have to work with 'UO' managers I try to supply the stability they so obviously lack. In my experience, if they are allowed to have too much of their own way, the management team's cohesion and order is threatened. I agree that on occasions they can come up with good ideas but I dislike the risks they always seem to want to take.

The 'UO' Manager

I think it is important for me as a manager to challenge the traditional approaches to problem-solving and decision-making in my organisation. If there are too many established norms and customs the organisation's progress will be slowed down. When decision-making and problem-solving I tend to look for answers wherever they can be found. Experience has taught me to consider the total situation in which the problem is set to find the best solution.

I enjoy problem-solving and like finding new and often different ways for doing things. My approach is often regarded as impractical but this does not bother me. I have rarely found that the views of the majority provide the best solution. For this reason if I am sure I have the right answer I usually go ahead regardless of what others think.

People in my organisation know that I am the manager to turn to in a crisis and I usually spot problems ahead of other people. Because I do not readily conform and sometimes adopt a carefree attitude, some of my seniors have suggested that I lack discipline. Although I don't agree with such statements I do find it difficult to follow routines for any length of time and try to avoid getting bogged down in too much detail. I regard change as the necessary catalyst for success.

When I have to work with 'O' managers I try to introduce new ideas and get them to break with the past. This approach sometimes leads to conflicts but I consider it my mission to stop them treating the means as the ends within the organisation. I have noticed that when my ideas are accepted they soon regard them as their own.

MAC

DEVELOPMENT GUIDE 8

The Watts-Manager's-Approach-to-Creativity indicator

Please read these notes very carefully before trying to answer any of the questions on the following pages.

INTRODUCING MAC I want you to think very carefully about the way you *like* to manage. All managers have their own approach to managing; for example, you may like to delay decisions until you have all the information, or keep your team on its toes by regularly changing routines. One thing is certain: there is no one best way to manage. MAC is not a test for which there is a right and a wrong way to respond. MAC is a development tool designed to help you gain more understanding of how you use the important management skill of creativity when you are managing.

COMPLETING MAC MAC consists of a list of forty-two statements. For each statement there are five possible words that can be used in the middle of the statement to complete it; for example:

I AM A MANAGER WHO IS usually—often—sometimes—seldom—rarely *PATIENT AND UNDERSTANDING WHEN DEALING WITH STAFF DISPUTES.*

You should complete the statement by ringing the word which, you feel, completes the statement in a way which is closest to your approach to managing. Only ring one word; for example:

I AM A MANAGER WHO IS usually—often—sometimes—seldom—rarely *PATIENT AND UNDERSTANDING WHEN DEALING WITH STAFF DISPUTES.*

When you have completed all the statements, total up your scores under the three separate trait headings and then total up the three traits to obtain your overall score; for example:

Traits	ID	OP	OC	usually	often	sometimes	seldom	rarely
(1) OP	3	⊔⊔⊔	⊔⊔⊔	1	2	③	4	5
(2) OC	⊔⊔⊔	4	⊔⊔⊔	5	④	3	2	1
(3) ID	2	⊔⊔⊔	⊔⊔⊔	5	4	3	②	1

There are no right or wrong answers and low marks are just as significant as high marks. An assessment of each of your trait scores and your overall score can be found by looking up the appendix.

MAC

DEVELOPMENT GUIDE 8

The Watts-Manager's-Approach-to-Creativity indicator

NAME: DATE:

(1) *I AM A MANAGER WHO* usually—often—sometimes—seldom—rarely *CHECKS DETAILS TO ENSURE THEY ARE CORRECT.*

(2) *I AM A MANAGER WHO* usually—often—sometimes—seldom—rarely *FOLLOWS COMPANY POLICY.*

(3) *I AM A MANAGER WHO* usually—often—sometimes—seldom—rarely *THINKS OF A SOLUTION IN A CRISIS.*

(4) *I AM A MANAGER WHO IS* usually—often—sometimes—seldom—rarely *FASTIDIOUS WHEN IT COMES TO DETAILED WORK.*

(5) *I AM A MANAGER WHO* usually—often—sometimes—seldom—rarely *PREFERS CREATING THINGS TO IMPROVING THINGS.*

(6) *I AM A MANAGER WHO* usually—often—sometimes—seldom—rarely *NEEDS THE PRECISE FACTS TO MAKE A DECISION.*

(7) *I AM A MANAGER WHO IS* usually—often—sometimes—seldom—rarely *RESPECTFUL OF HIGHER AUTHORITY.*

(8) *I AM A MANAGER WHO* usually—often—sometimes—seldom—rarely *THINKS UP NEW IDEAS.*

(9) *I AM A MANAGER WHO* usually—often—sometimes—seldom—rarely *BREAKS OR BENDS THE RULES.*

(10) *I AM A MANAGER WHO* usually—often—sometimes—seldom—rarely *LIKES TO WORK WITHIN A STRUCTURED OPERATING ENVIRONMENT.*

(11) *I AM A MANAGER WHO* usually—often—sometimes—seldom—rarely *LIKES TO DISCUSS MY IDEAS WITH SUPERIORS.*

(12) *I AM A MANAGER WHO* usually—often—sometimes—seldom—rarely *HAS A SET PATTERN OF WORKING.*

(13) *I AM A MANAGER WHO* usually—often—sometimes—seldom—rarely *DEVELOPS NEW APPROACHES TO LONG-STANDING PROBLEMS.*

(14) *I AM A MANAGER WHO* usually—often—sometimes—seldom—rarely *CONSIDERS ALL THE EVIDENCE BEFORE TAKING ACTION.*

(15) *I AM A MANAGER WHO* usually—often—sometimes—seldom—rarely *NEEDS TO BE GIVEN TIME TO ADAPT TO CHANGES.*

(16) *I AM A MANAGER WHO IS* usually—often—sometimes—seldom—rarely *REGARDED AS METHODICAL AND SYSTEMATIC.*

(17) *I AM A MANAGER WHO* usually—often—sometimes—seldom—rarely *PREFERS TO WORK AT A STEADY PACE.*

(18) *I AM A MANAGER WHO* usually—often—sometimes—seldom—rarely *ENJOYS COPING WITH LOTS OF NEW IDEAS AND PROBLEMS AT ONCE.*

(19) *I AM A MANAGER WHO* usually—often—sometimes—seldom—rarely *ACTS IN A WAY THAT IS CONSISTENT WITHIN THE ORGANISATION.*

(20) *I AM A MANAGER WHO* usually—often—sometimes—seldom—rarely *WILL GO IT ALONE IF I BELIEVE I AM RIGHT.*

(21) *I AM A MANAGER WHO* usually—often—sometimes—seldom—rarely *LIKES TO FOLLOW A PLANNED WORK PROGRAMME.*

MAC

DEVELOPMENT GUIDE 8

The Watts-Manager's-Approach-to-Creativity indicator

NAME: _____ DATE: _____

(22) *I AM A MANAGER WHO* usually—often—sometimes—seldom—rarely *STIMULATES THE TEAM.*

(23) *I AM A MANAGER WHO IS* usually—often—sometimes—seldom—rarely *RESPECTFUL OF MAJORITY VIEWS.*

(24) *I AM A MANAGER WHO* usually—often—sometimes—seldom—rarely *HAS IDEAS OF AN ORIGINAL QUALITY.*

(25) *I AM A MANAGER WHO* usually—often—sometimes—seldom—rarely *ACTS ONLY WITHIN GIVEN AUTHORITY.*

(26) *I AM A MANAGER WHO* usually—often—sometimes—seldom—rarely *PAYS A LOT OF ATTENTION TO DETAIL.*

(27) *I AM A MANAGER WHO* usually—often—sometimes—seldom—rarely *PREFERS TO DELEGATE THE DETAILED WORK.*

(28) *I AM A MANAGER WHO* usually—often—sometimes—seldom—rarely *PREFERS TO WORK TO A LAID-DOWN PROCEDURE.*

(29) *I AM A MANAGER WHO* usually—often—sometimes—seldom—rarely *DEALS WITH PROBLEMS ONE AT A TIME.*

(30) *I AM A MANAGER WHO* usually—often—sometimes—seldom—rarely *HAS A CONSISTENT APPROACH TO WORK.*

(31) *I AM A MANAGER WHO IS* usually—often—sometimes—seldom—rarely *PREPARED TO RISK DOING THINGS DIFFERENTLY.*

(32) *I AM A MANAGER WHO* usually—often—sometimes—seldom—rarely *SUPPORTS 'MANAGEMENT BY EXCEPTION'.*

(33) *I AM A MANAGER WHO* usually—often—sometimes—seldom—rarely *WORKS TO ESTABLISHED NORMS.*

(34) *I AM A MANAGER WHO* usually—often—sometimes—seldom—rarely *IMPOSES A STRICT ORDER ON THINGS UNDER MY CONTROL.*

(35) *I AM A MANAGER WHO* usually—often—sometimes—seldom—rarely *READILY ADAPTS TO CHANGE.*

(36) *I AM A MANAGER WHO* usually—often—sometimes—seldom—rarely *LIKES TO WORK WITH PRECISE INSTRUCTIONS.*

(37) *I AM A MANAGER WHO IS* usually—often—sometimes—seldom—rarely *COMFORTABLE WITHIN 'THE SYSTEM'.*

(38) *I AM A MANAGER WHO* usually—often—sometimes—seldom—rarely *DOES THINGS IN A LOGICAL SEQUENCE.*

(39) *I AM A MANAGER WHO IS* usually—often—sometimes—seldom—rarely *STIMULATED BY CHANGING DEMANDS.*

(40) *I AM A MANAGER WHO* usually—often—sometimes—seldom—rarely *SEEKS COMPREHENSIVE INSTRUCTIONS.*

(41) *I AM A MANAGER WHO* usually—often—sometimes—seldom—rarely *NEEDS PEERS WHO MAINTAIN THE 'STATUS QUO'.*

(42) *I AM A MANAGER WHO* usually—often—sometimes—seldom—rarely *HAS LOTS OF IDEAS ON PROBLEM SITUATIONS.*

MAC

DEVELOPMENT GUIDE 8

The Watts-Manager's-Approach-to-Creativity indicator

TRAITS	1D	OP	OC	usually	often	SCORE sometimes	seldom	rarely
(1) OP				1	2	3	4	5
(2) OC				1	2	3	4	5
(3) ID				5	4	3	2	1
(4) OP				1	2	3	4	5
(5) ID				5	4	3	2	1
(6) OP				1	2	3	4	5
(7) OC				1	2	3	4	5
(8) ID				5	4	3	2	1
(9) OC				5	4	3	2	1
(10) OC				1	2	3	4	5
(11) OC				1	2	3	4	5
(12) OP				1	2	3	4	5
(13) ID				5	4	3	2	1
(14) OP				1	2	3	4	5
(15) ID				1	2	3	4	5
(16) OP				1	2	3	4	5
(17) OP				1	2	3	4	5
(18) ID				5	4	3	2	1
(19) OC				1	2	3	4	5
(20) ID				5	4	3	2	1
(21) OP				1	2	3	4	5
C/F TOTAL	ID	OP	OC	= C/F OVERALL TOTAL				

MAC

DEVELOPMENT GUIDE 8

The Watts-Manager's-Approach-to-Creativity indicator

TRAITS	1D	OP	OC	usually	often	SCORE sometimes	seldom	rarely
(22) ID				5	4	3	2	1
(23) OC				1	2	3	4	5
(24) ID				5	4	3	2	1
(25) OC				1	2	3	4	5
(26) OP				1	2	3	4	5
(27) OP				5	4	3	2	1
(28) OC				1	2	3	4	5
(29) ID				1	2	3	4	5
(30) OP				1	2	3	4	5
(31) ID				5	4	3	2	1
(32) OP				5	4	3	2	1
(33) OC				1	2	3	4	5
(34) OP				1	2	3	4	5
(35) ID				5	4	3	2	1
(36) OC				1	2	3	4	5
(37) OC				1	2	3	4	5
(38) OP				1	2	3	4	5
(39) ID				5	4	3	2	1
(40) OC				1	2	3	4	5
(41) OC				1	2	3	4	5
(42) ID				5	4	3	2	1
C/F TOTAL	ID	OP	OC	= C/F OVERALL TOTAL				

MANAGERIAL APTITUDE MEASUREMENT

I hope completing **MAC** and checking the results has convinced you of the value of personality and aptitude assessment. I am now going to suggest that you take another assessment, this time to measure your aptitude. There is a difference between personality and aptitude assessments. Personality assessments measure what you are and how you will tend to behave. The results are neither good nor bad but they may predict behaviour that is inappropriate or appropriate in certain situations. Aptitude assessments measure the level of power or skill to do something that you have in comparison with other people. Those people may be a specific population such as managers or a general population. The results of an aptitude assessment can have a negative effect, especially if they are poor in comparison with the population you are comparing the person with. If you are faced with this problem remember the individual concerned will improve with development and act accordingly.

The next assessment was also written by me and is called The Watts-Manager's Assessment of Thinking Effectiveness, **MATE** for short.

WHAT MATE IS ALL ABOUT

MATE has been specifically designed to enable you and your managers to gain a greater understanding of the effectiveness of their managerial thinking. That is the thinking they need to apply when dealing with managerial decision making and problem solving. **MATE** consists of four assessments each of which tests a slightly different aspect of a manager's thinking effectiveness. The assessments should take less than one hour to complete.

I strongly recommend that you measure your own performance with **MATE** before getting your managers to do it. You will then be able to use your own reactions to the results as a guide for approaching the feedback process.

If you intend to assess a lot of managers, the results of **MATE** can be used to develop an organisational population. You will be able to use the data collected for your population to compare the results with those of new managerial job applicants. This will enable you to ensure that you only employ people with the levels of thinking effectiveness your organisation needs.

MATE is an ideal development measuring tool. If you are sending managers on development programmes or running in-company development programmes, you should consider using **MATE** both at the beginning and end of the programme. Most good programmes will show an improvement in thinking effectiveness.

One problem that arises as a result of including assessments such as

MATE in a book like this is that everyone has access to the answers. To overcome this you can obtain purpose-designed copies with different questions and answers. These can be obtained via the follow-up service detailed in the appendix. Through this service you will be able to purchase sets of **MATE** questions complete with a computer program. The program will run on any IBM compatible computer that will accept MS-DOS 2.11, and will generate individual reports/recommendations, create a database of results and analyse the collective data. This service is available to all qualified management developers.

The **MATE** assessments are laid out as Development Guide 9. Each assessment is preceded by a set of instructions.

DISCOVERY EXERCISE

Do MATE. *Allow 45–60 minutes.*

When you have completed and marked your own **MATE** assessments you can check what your scores mean by turning to the appendix.

MATE   DEVELOPMENT GUIDE 9

The Watts-Manager's Assessment of Thinking Effectiveness (MATE)

INTRODUCING MATE The Watts-Manager's Assessment of Thinking Effectiveness is a set of four assessments based on the thinking aptitudes you, as a manager, might be required to display when you are dealing with managerial tasks.

The assessments assess your ability to make conclusions and evaluations regarding problems and information requiring managerial action.

The assessments cover arguments, assumptions, deductions, inductions and inferences. All the assessments are based on business and organisational situations which should be familiar to you as a manager operating in the free world.

COMPLETING MATE The assessments require you to answer 72 questions as follows:

ASSESSMENT ONE Assumptions (4 statements–16 questions): assesses your ability to recognise the unstated assumptions made in statements during discussions.

ASSESSMENT TWO Deduction (4 statements–16 questions): assesses your ability to reason things out from general situations and statements that may be made or quoted, to arrive at specific and correct conclusions.

ASSESSMENT THREE Arguments (4 propositions–16 questions): assesses your ability to recognise the value in arguments, either in support or opposition to proposed managerial decisions, regardless of your own viewpoint.

ASSESSMENT FOUR Induction and inference (3 paragraphs–18 questions): assesses your ability to handle data from various sources and differentiate between what can definitely be induced and what is, to a varying extent or degree, inferred.

These four assess your thinking effectiveness, not the speed at which you can respond so there is no formal time limit. Most managers are able to complete the assessments in about 45 minutes. You should try to manage your time when taking the assessments as follows:

| ONE | *assumptions:* | 12 mins. | TWO | *deduction:* | 10 mins. |
| THREE | *arguments:* | 9 mins. | FOUR | *induction/inference:* | 14 mins. |

Each assessment is on a separate pair of pages with accompanying scoring pages which should not be viewed until completion of the assessment. When you have read this page and are satisfied that you understand the purpose and approximate timing of the assessments you should read the instructions for Assessment One and then begin.

MATE

DEVELOPMENT GUIDE 9

ASSESSMENT ONE: ASSUMPTIONS

Managers have to make assumptions a lot of the time: it is not possible for a really effective manager to double-check everything that everyone is doing in every detail. When a trusted and reliable member of your team says, 'I will see the ABC company next month to finalise the terms of next year's contract' you are likely to assume, from the statement, that the ABC company is now ready to finalise the contract and that your staff member knows the right person to see on the right day.

In the assessment you are now going to undertake there are four statements. Each is followed by four possible assumptions that could be made from that statement. Your task is to decide which of the assumptions are taken for granted in the statement. Study the example provided below and when you understand what is required start work on the assumption assessment pages. Read each assumption in conjunction with the statement and then simply ring the word CORRECT or INCORRECT.

For example:

STATEMENT
'My analysis suggests that the majority of successful Japanese managers spend most of their business life working for the one employer.'

POSSIBLE ASSUMPTIONS

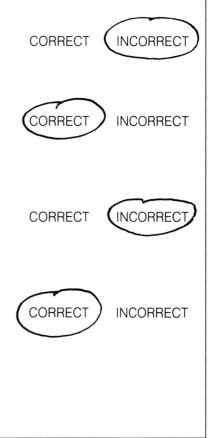

(1) If you work for one employer for a long time you will be successful.

CORRECT   INCORRECT

The assumption is incorrect because the statement is specific to Japanese management.

(2) Loyalty is a necessary ingredient for success in Japanese management.

CORRECT   INCORRECT

The assumption is correct because long service implies loyalty and the majority of successful Japanese managers have long service records.

(3) You can learn more about being a successful manager if you stay with one employer.

CORRECT   INCORRECT

The assumption is incorrect because the statement makes no reference either directly or indirectly to the learning process.

(4) Japanese employers usually promote people into management positions who have been with them a long time.

CORRECT   INCORRECT

The assumption is correct because it is stated that successful Japanese managers are long-term employees.

Now start work on the assumption skills assessment pages.

MATE

DEVELOPMENT GUIDE 9

ASSESSMENT ONE: ASSUMPTIONS

STATEMENT ONE
'It is essential for you all to realise that the raw materials supplier's distribution costs have a signifi-cant bearing on the final cost of all the products in the market, both ours and our competitors.'

ASSUMPTIONS

(1) Collecting directly from the supplier will reduce the final cost of the product we make.   CORRECT   INCORRECT

(2) The further away our supplier is the more expensive their supplies will be.   CORRECT   INCORRECT

(3) Buying supplies in bulk will reduce their cost.   CORRECT   INCORRECT

(4) Buying from the same supplier as a competitor is not necessarily a disadvantage.   CORRECT   INCORRECT

STATEMENT TWO
'These consumer protection laws are not always a bad thing; they often increase opportunities for the businesses that concentrate on producing high-quality and expensive products.'

ASSUMPTIONS

(1) Cheap products do not meet the requirements of the laws related to consumer protection.   CORRECT   INCORRECT

(2) Careful customers only buy high-quality products.   CORRECT   INCORRECT

(3) The more expensive a product is, the more likely it is to comply with consumer protection laws.   CORRECT   INCORRECT

(4) Consumer protection laws can have a positive as well as negative effect on a business if it thinks about the consequences of their introduction.   CORRECT   INCORRECT

MATE

DEVELOPMENT GUIDE 9

STATEMENT THREE

'I say that the only reason why people go to work is to get money. Money has and always will be what people really go to work for.'

ASSUMPTIONS

(1) Job satisfaction is not important to people.	CORRECT	INCORRECT
(2) The more money you give people the harder they will work.	CORRECT	INCORRECT
(3) People will not generally work for you unless they receive money for what they do.	CORRECT	INCORRECT
(4) The best way to get people to do things for you is to offer them money.	CORRECT	INCORRECT

STATEMENT FOUR

'Without doubt capital is the key to business success: more businesses fail because of lack of capital than for any other reason.'

ASSUMPTIONS

(1) Without the right amount of capital a business cannot succeed.	CORRECT	INCORRECT
(2) All successful businesses were capitalised with large sums of money.	CORRECT	INCORRECT
(3) Under capitalisation is a major reason for business failure.	CORRECT	INCORRECT
(4) Before you start a business you should ensure that you have adequate capital.	CORRECT	INCORRECT

MATE

DEVELOPMENT GUIDE 9

ASSESSMENT ONE: ASSUMPTIONS (SCORESHEET)

	SCORE	
	CORRECT	INCORRECT
STATEMENT ONE		
Assumption (1)	0	1
Assumption (2)	0	1
Assumption (3)	0	1
Assumption (4)	1	0
STATEMENT TWO		
Assumption (1)	0	1
Assumption (2)	0	1
Assumption (3)	1	0
Assumption (4)	1	0

Total assumptions C/F_____

MATE

DEVELOPMENT GUIDE 9

ASSESSMENT ONE: ASSUMPTIONS (SCORESHEET)

	SCORE	
	CORRECT	INCORRECT
STATEMENT THREE		
Assumption (1)	1	0
Assumption (2)	0	1
Assumption (3)	1	0
Assumption (4)	1	0
STATEMENT FOUR		
Assumption (1)	1	0
Assumption (2)	0	1
Assumption (3)	1	0
Assumption (4)	0	1

Total assumptions_____

MATE

DEVELOPMENT GUIDE 9

ASSESSMENT TWO: DEDUCTION

The ability to make deductions from information provided is a necessary managerial skill. Deduction skills are, in essence, those skills of thinking effectively that enable you, as a manager, to arrive at specific and correct conclusions from general information by reasoning.

In the assessment you are now about to undertake there are four statements. You should assume, for the purposes of this assessment, that each statement is true. For each statement there are four sets of conclusions; you are required to decide which of the conclusions that have been reached are reasonable and which are unreasonable. Study the example provided below and when you understand what is required start work on the deduction assessment. Read each conclusion in conjunction with the statement and then simply ring the word REASONABLE or UNREASONABLE.
For example:

STATEMENT
'To be really successful in your own business you must first believe in yourself and your ability to overcome the many difficulties that arise from starting and running your own company.'

CONCLUSIONS
Therefore:
(1) It is likely that people who do not have self-confidence will find it difficult to be successful in their own business.   ~~REASONABLE~~ UNREASONABLE

The statement says that self-belief is needed to be really successful in business so the conclusion is reasonable.

(2) Most successful business people experience near-failure on their route to owning a successful business.   REASONABLE ~~UNREASONABLE~~

Although the statement suggests that difficulties will occur it does not contain any evidence that most successful people experience near failure on their way to success, so the conclusion is unreasonable.

(3) It is very difficult to start your own business unless you have special abilities.   REASONABLE ~~UNREASONABLE~~

There is nothing in the statement to suggest that special abilities are required to start your own business, so the conclusion is unreasonable.

(4) People who have a lot of belief in their own abilities usually prefer to own their own businesses.   REASONABLE ~~UNREASONABLE~~

The statement is concerned with success in business and the foundations for that success. A link with self-belief is established but only in the context of the foundations for success, not as a preference for business ownership, so the conclusion is unreasonable.

Now start work on the deduction skills assessment pages.

MATE

DEVELOPMENT GUIDE 9

STATEMENT ONE

'In most organisations skilled shop floor workers enjoy better pay and working conditions than unskilled shop floor workers; office staff enjoy even better working conditions.'

CONCLUSIONS

Therefore:

(1) It is always better to be a worker in an office than it is to be a shop floor worker.　　REASONABLE　UNREASONABLE

(2) To be able to earn the same wages as skilled workers, unskilled workers need to work overtime.　　REASONABLE　UNREASONABLE

(3) Office staff do not have to work overtime and have longer holidays than skilled shop-floor workers.　　REASONABLE　UNREASONABLE

(4) Skilled workers enjoy working conditions that are different from unskilled workers and office staff.　　REASONABLE　UNREASONABLE

STATEMENT TWO

'In 1929 40% of the businesses in the USA went broke. 30% of the businesses that went broke were related to agriculture; and 25% of the banks that closed did so because they could not realise on the farms and agricultural land they had taken as security for the loans they advanced.'

CONCLUSIONS

Therefore:

(1) Farmers were the biggest single group of bankrupt businesses in 1929 in the USA.　　REASONABLE　UNREASONABLE

(2) More banks in the USA went bankrupt due to agriculture than any other activity in 1929.　　REASONABLE　UNREASONABLE

(3) Lending money to agricultural-related businesses proved to be a very bad risk for a major part of the USA banking sector in 1929.　　REASONABLE　UNREASONABLE

(4) A high percentage of the USA's industrial businesses failed in the 1929 crash. Their failure was due in part to the banks trying to call in loans.　　REASONABLE　UNREASONABLE

MATE

DEVELOPMENT GUIDE 9

STATEMENT THREE

'Advertising is the most widely used tool in the promotion of fast-moving consumer goods while personal selling is the most widely used tool in the selling of industrial durables.'

CONCLUSIONS

Therefore:

(1) Advertising is not normally a significant factor in the promotion of most industrial durables.   REASONABLE   UNREASONABLE

(2) People prefer not to be bothered by sales personnel when they are out shopping.   REASONABLE   UNREASONABLE

(3) Personal selling and advertising are two of the tools available to companies wishing to promote their products.   REASONABLE   UNREASONABLE

(4) Customers are made aware of fast-moving consumer goods via the media rather than personal introduction.   REASONABLE   UNREASONABLE

STATEMENT FOUR

'Transportation costs have risen faster than any other organisation costs over the last ten years. More and more organisations are giving up their own transport in favour of using outside companies as and when they need them.'

CONCLUSIONS

Therefore:

(1) The biggest on-cost for most products is transportation.   REASONABLE   UNREASONABLE

(2) Distribution costs can be cut by using outside transport companies rather than one's own transport.   REASONABLE   UNREASONABLE

(3) Most products are more expensive than they were ten years ago because of higher transport costs.   REASONABLE   UNREASONABLE

(4) Controlling transport costs is a primary consideration of management.   REASONABLE   UNREASONABLE

MATE

DEVELOPMENT GUIDE 9

ASSESSMENT TWO: DEDUCTION (SCORESHEET)

	SCORE	
	REASONABLE	UNREASONABLE
STATEMENT ONE		
Conclusion (1)	0	1
Conclusion (2)	1	0
Conclusion (3)	0	1
Conclusion (4)	1	0
STATEMENT TWO		
Conclusion (1)	0	1
Conclusion (2)	0	1
Conclusion (3)	1	0
Conclusion (4)	0	1

Total deduction C/F_____

MATE

DEVELOPMENT GUIDE 9

ASSESSMENT TWO: DEDUCTION (SCORESHEET)

	SCORE	
	REASONABLE	UNREASONABLE
STATEMENT THREE		
Conclusion (1)	1	0
Conclusion (2)	0	1
Conclusion (3)	1	0
Conclusion (4)	1	0
STATEMENT FOUR		
Conclusion (1)	0	1
Conclusion (2)	1	0
Conclusion (3)	0	1
Conclusion (4)	1	0

Total deduction_____

MATE
DEVELOPMENT GUIDE 9

ASSESSMENT THREE: ARGUMENTS

The evaluation and assessment of arguments made either in support of or in opposition to proposed decisions within an organisation is a key managerial task. All managers need to be able to recognise the value in an argument even if they hold the opposite view and therefore, might find it uncomfortable to do so.

In the assessment you are now about to undertake four questions requiring managerial attention are posed. For each question four arguments are presented; you should assume for the purposes of this assessment that all the arguments are true. You are required to assess each argument and decide, regardless of whether you agree with the argument or not, whether it is valid. Study the example provided below and when you understand what is required start work on the arguments assessment. Read each argument in conjunction with the question and simply ring the words VALID or NOT VALID.
For example:

QUESTION
'Should we check to ensure all aspects of our operations comply with the most stringent health and safety at work regulations, even though we have no dangerous machinery and have not been told we must?'

(1) 'YES: today's workers are entitled to expect that their employers will look after all aspects of their welfare while they are at work.'   VALID   ⬭NOT VALID⬭

This argument states the employees' general expectations of their employers regarding safety, but does not directly address the question. All aspects of the employees' welfare may indeed already be looked after; the question asks whether a non-mandatory check should be made. The argument is therefore not valid.

(2) 'NO: it is unnecessary, no authority has asked for access to inspect and it is unlikely that they will. Remember we are not the type of business the authorities normally have trouble with.'   ⬭VALID⬭   NOT VALID

This argument does address the question and provides information which suggests no problems will arise by not checking. It is therefore a valid argument.

(3) 'NO: the people we employ are not fools, they should be responsible for themselves and their own actions while they are going about their work.'   VALID   ⬭NOT VALID⬭

This argument again does not address the question. No question was posed suggesting that employees should be responsible for their own safety. It is therefore not a valid argument.

(4) 'NO: if we try introducing extra rules and regulations it will inhibit our employees' innovation in finding new ways of doing things.'   VALID   ⬭NOT VALID⬭

The argument may be true but the question does not refer to the problem of complying with the regulations; it refers to a non-mandatory check so the argument is not valid.

Now start work on the evaluation of arguments assessment.

MATE DEVELOPMENT GUIDE 9

QUESTION ONE

'Should we go ahead and accept this government contract even though it means tying up a large part of the work force on work that will only give us a very small profit return?'

(1) 'YES: we could probably use the work over the next twelve months and I expect it will save us spending lots of money trying to sell our services elsewhere.'	VALID	NOT VALID
(2) NO: nobody ever got rich working on government contracts and by the time we have waited for the money we are likely to make a loss.'	VALID	NOT VALID
(3) 'YES: if we do well on this contract there will be others that could lead to us becoming established government contractors.'	VALID	NOT VALID
(4) 'YES: all our competitors are trying to get government contracts; they know work is going to be short for a while. I want us to go ahead: my people think we can cut our costs if we try hard enough.	VALID	NOT VALID

QUESTION TWO

'Should we employ the young candidate with all the qualifications, even though he has only worked for one other organisation or should we wait and see if we can hire an older person with a longer track record. Remember this is a senior position dealing with important customers.'

(1) 'YES: go ahead. This organisation needs young people in senior positions; they can always learn on the job.'	VALID	NOT VALID
(2) 'NO: in our business it is experience that counts; our customers look to us to handle the difficulties connected with foreign currencies. Only someone with experience will be able to deal with such tasks.'	VALID	NOT VALID
(3) 'YES: we haven't seen anybody better all day and we can't afford to spend another day sitting here seeing people hoping to find someone with more experience.'	VALID	NOT VALID
(4) 'NO: we have always put the needs of the customer first when selecting someone for this type of job. Now we are being asked to change our selection criteria for the sake of expediency. I know this person is well qualified on paper but I for one don't feel comfortable about appointing him.'	VALID	NOT VALID

MATE

DEVELOPMENT GUIDE 9

QUESTION THREE

'Should we move the stores from their current central position to the new town? Remember if we do it will enable us to realise on a large piece of real estate at a time when we are very short of hard cash.'

(1) 'YES: it's a good idea; with a little planning we should be able to service everyone just as we did before.'	VALID	NOT VALID
(2) 'NO: at the moment prices are not that good for central sites. I think we should wait until the market picks up before we sell.'	VALID	NOT VALID
(3) 'YES: we need a new store's layout and moving would give us an ideal opportunity to do so.'	VALID	NOT VALID
(4) 'NO: the time it will take to sell will be too long and the disruption plus the delay will wipe out any financial advantage.'	VALID	NOT VALID

QUESTION FOUR

'Should we go ahead now with the installation of a new mini-computer system as consultants recommend? A new super-micro system might give us more advantages once the suppliers finalise the software packages for it.'

(1) 'NO: we should wait because we want the latest technology so we can remain ahead.'	VALID	NOT VALID
(2) 'YES: we know that the mini will be adequate for the next five years; waiting for the latest and greatest will give us no extra advantages.'	VALID	NOT VALID
(3) 'YES: we should not employ a consultant and then ignore their advice; it's a waste of time and money if we do.'	VALID	NOT VALID
(4) 'NO: we should wait for the super-micro: it will give us cost advantages long-term, the software is likely to be cheaper and the hardware more flexible and user friendly.'	VALID	NOT VALID

MATE

DEVELOPMENT GUIDE 9

ASSESSMENT THREE: ARGUMENTS (SCORESHEET)

	SCORE	
	VALID	NOT VALID
QUESTION ONE		
Option (1)	0	1
Option (2)	0	1
Option (3)	1	0
Option (4)	1	0
QUESTION TWO		
Option (1)	0	1
Option (2)	1	0
Option (3)	0	1
Option (4)	1	0

Total arguments C/F_____

MATE

DEVELOPMENT GUIDE 9

ASSESSMENT THREE: ARGUMENTS (SCORESHEET)

	SCORE	
	VALID	NOT VALID
QUESTION THREE		
Option (1)	1	0
Option (2)	1	0
Option (3)	0	1
Option (4)	1	0
QUESTION FOUR		
Option (1)	0	1
Option (2)	1	0
Option (3)	0	1
Option (4)	1	0

Total arguments_____

MATE

DEVELOPMENT GUIDE 9

ASSESSMENT FOUR: INDUCTION AND INFERENCE

INDUCTION

Induction refers to the process of making, from the details and circumstances surrounding a particular situation, conclusions which, without doubt or at least much doubt, would apply generally. Such conclusions are *induced*.

INFERENCE

Inference refers to the process of weighing evidence and arriving at conclusions which are more speculative, but which may also apply, to a greater or lesser extent or degree, generally. Such conclusions are *inferred*.

   The ability to handle data from various sources and differentiate between what can definitely be *induced* and what is, to a various extent or degree, *inferred* is a skill required by managers. This skill is necessary for successful managerial decision-making.

For example:
If, as a manager, you were told that experiments with a voice recognition word processor had proved 100% successful, that twenty selected companies were using them without any problems and that savings on the cost of data transmission were at least 40%. It would be:

(1) Reasonable to conclude, *without doubt*, that all organisations and individuals, having a use for word processing in general, could benefit from such equipment.

(2) Reasonable to conclude, *without much doubt*, that a very large number of organisations and individuals would, sooner or later, want to benefit from such equipment.

(3) Reasonable to conclude, *to a large extent*, that new users would not experience too many problems with the equipment.

(4) Possible to conclude, *to some extent*, that traditional word-processing methods would, over a period of time, become obsolete.

(5) Possible to conclude, *to a degree*, that typists would lose their jobs and commercial schools lose their customers.

(6) Possible *to speculate* that all managers would do their own typing.

The assessment you are now going to take requires you to read three paragraphs. Assume, for the purposes of this assessment, that the content of each paragraph is true. For each paragraph there are six possible general conclusions. Your task is to decide which of these general conclusions is established:

(1) without doubt	**(2)** without much doubt	**(3)** to a large extent
(4) to some extent	**(5)** to a degree	**(6)** speculatively only

Study again the example provided above and when you understand what is required start work on the induction and inference assessment. Read each paragraph in conjunction with the conclusions and simply ring the numbers 1 2 3 4 5 or 6.

Now start work on the induction and inference assessment pages.

MATE

DEVELOPMENT GUIDE 9

STATEMENT ONE

All of the leading banks will compete with each other to lend money to a company that can offer freehold land as a fixed asset security for the loan. Banks traditionally like things they can easily realise on and which don't lose their value as security. Specialised machinery, stock and transport can be used but these are not so attractive to the banks. It is doubtful whether you would be able to get more than 40% of the value of such items as a loan.

(1) Land is the most valuable fixed asset a business can own.

1 2 3 4 5 6

(2) Most banks will accept land as security for a loan.

1 2 3 4 5 6

(3) Offering land as security is the best way to get a competitive bank loan.

1 2 3 4 5 6

(4) It is possible to use machinery, stock and buildings as security for a bank loan.

1 2 3 4 5 6

(5) Most banks are reluctant to lend money up to the maximum value of that which is offered as security.

1 2 3 4 5 6

(6) Banks never lend money without some form of security unless you have a good track record with the bank for paying back loans.

1 2 3 4 5 6

STATEMENT TWO

When Frederick Herzberg first introduced his theory on motivation an article appeared by a famous Columbia professor claiming that Herzberg did not believe in money as a means of getting people to perform. Although Herzberg denied that this was the basis of his theory, problems keep arising from the article. For a long while he received many requests from people asking him to act as a management consultant on the basis of the article. In the end Herzberg increased his fees to correct the situation.

(1) Herzberg does not consider that money is a motivator.

1 2 3 4 5 6

(2) Many companies were looking for a motivation theory that would increase productivity without increasing their wages bill.

1 2 3 4 5 6

(3) Herzberg increased his fees to prove that money was a very important component in the productivity and performance equation.

1 2 3 4 5 6

(4) The Columbia professor had created lots of work for Herzberg and had enabled him to put up his fees.

1 2 3 4 5 6

(5) Herzberg's theory was so confusing that even a university professor could not interpret it correctly.

1 2 3 4 5 6

(6) High fees enabled Herzberg to prove his theory to a lot of people.

1 2 3 4 5 6

MATE   DEVELOPMENT GUIDE 9

STATEMENT THREE
A study of the reasons for the success of some companies in establishing overseas subsidiaries and the failure of others claims that those having their own corporate culture are more likely to succeed. The study found that in most instances the companies that have implanted their own corporate culture, rather than trying to adapt to the existing cultures of the community, have experienced long-term success. Each of the successful companies was said to have spent a long period of time selecting and training local people in the ways of their corporations. They had in each instance set out to get the people to give their first allegiance to the corporation rather than the society. The most successful claimed that they had made no concessions for local culture and that all staff were sent regularly to the company's home base for long periods of training.

CONCLUSIONS

(1) The companies had shown the right way to set up businesses overseas.

1 2 3 4 5 6

(2) The companies, via the development of a corporate culture, had overcome all the difficulties experienced with setting up operations overseas.

1 2 3 4 5 6

(3) The companies claim that there is good evidence that corporate cultural development is the right way to overcome the cultural differences that exist in multi-nationals.

1 2 3 4 5 6

(4) The companies think sending new staff for training to the companies' HQs introduces the staff to new cultural influences that they prefer to their own.

1 2 3 4 5 6

(5) The good working conditions and job prospects found in multinational companies make staff change their cultural commitments.

1 2 3 4 5 6

(6) Selecting the right people for the job and then spending a lot of time training them in the ways of the company is advocated by the successful companies.

1 2 3 4 5 6

MATE

DEVELOPMENT GUIDE 9

ASSESSMENT FOUR:
INDUCTION AND INFERENCE
(SCORESHEET)

	without doubt	without much doubt	to a large extent	to some extent	to a degree	speculatively only
STATEMENT ONE						
Option (1)	0	0	1	2	1	0
Option (2)	2	1	1	0	0	0
Option (3)	0	0	0	1	1	2
Option (4)	2	1	1	0	0	0
Option (5)	2	1	1	0	0	0
Option (6)	0	0	0	1	1	2
STATEMENT TWO						
Option (1)	1	1	2	0	0	0
Option (2)	1	2	1	0	0	0
Option (3)	1	2	1	0	0	0
Option (4)	0	0	1	2	1	0
Option (5)	0	0	0	1	1	2
Option (6)	0	0	0	1	1	2

Total induction and inferences C/F_____

MATE

DEVELOPMENT GUIDE 9

ASSESSMENT FOUR:
INDUCTION AND INFERENCE
(SCORESHEET)

	without doubt	without much doubt	to a large extent	to some extent	to a degree	speculatively only
STATEMENT THREE						
Option **(1)**	0	0	0	1	2	1
Option **(2)**	0	0	0	1	1	2
Option **(3)**	0	1	2	1	0	0
Option **(4)**	0	0	0	1	1	2
Option **(5)**	0	0	1	1	2	0
Option **(6)**	2	1	1	0	0	0

Total induction and inferences_____

BEHAVIOURAL AND MANAGERIAL PERFORMANCE

I hope you did not find MATE too demanding and still have some energy left to consider the next stage in the process of analysing the strengths and weaknesses of your management team. I now want to show you how you can look at the personality characteristics and behavioural tendencies of your managers in more detail.

THE 16PF ASSESSMENT

So far we have looked at your managers' thinking effectiveness and how they are likely to deploy creativity in the problem-solving process. The assessment we are now going to consider is capable of providing information on a manager's total personality; it is called the 16PF, Form A, Edition R. The 16PF can only be administered and interpreted by those who are professionally qualified to administer psychological assessments and my comments are based on having that qualification.

The 16PF was devised by an Englishman, now Professor Raymond B. Cattell. The 16 stands for the number of personality characteristics the assessment measures and the PF stands for personality factors.

The Cattell 16 personality factors were first introduced commercially in 1949 after 10 years of empirical, factor-analytic research. The personality factors measured by the 16PF are not just unique to the assessment, but instead are drawn from the generally accepted theory of personality. The 16PF has been used in over 3,000 published academic research studies on both normal and clinical groups. (IPAT) The Institute for Personality and Ability Testing, Inc., P.O. Box 188, Champaign, Illinois 61820-0188 is responsible for the distribution and development of the 16PF and the version we are going to look at was introduced by them in 1980. Figure 1 illustrates the primary source traits identified by the 16PF test.

The factors listed in Figure 1 have important implications for management development and later in the chapter they will be discussed. The important thing to remember when you are considering using the 16PF is that it is capable of providing you and each of your managers with a very comprehensive and objective personality assessment in a relatively short period of time.

Unfortunately it is not possible to reproduce the 16PF for general use in this book. The results of a 16PF require expert interpretation and this is only possible after a period of training. My objective in introducing you to the 16PF is to show you its benefits and to point you in the right direction for further information. When you have all the information you can then decide if using the 16PF is right for the development of your managers. I recommend it and find it an invaluable tool.

	Low score description							High score description		
					←*Average*→					
	1	2	3	4	5	6	7	8	9	10
FACTOR										
A	Autonomous–reserved							Participating–warm		
B	Concrete–thinking							Conceptual–thinking		
C	Affected by feelings							Calm–unruffled		
E	Considerate–humble							Assertive–competitive		
F	Reflective–serious							Talkative–impulsive		
G	Changeable–expedient							Persistent–conforming		
H	Cautious–shy							Socially bold		
I	Tough-minded							Tender-minded–sensitive		
L	Accepting–trusting							Mistrusting–oppositional		
M	Conventional–practical							Imaginative		
N	Forthright–unprentious							Sophisticated–shrewd		
O	Confident–self-assured							Apprehensive–concerned		
Q1	Conservative–traditional							Experimental–liberal		
Q2	Group-oriented							Self-sufficient		
Q3	Lax–uncontrolled							Disciplined–compulsive		
Q4	Composed–relaxed							Tense–driven		

FIG. 1. THE PRIMARY SOURCE TRAITS IDENTIFIED BY THE 16PF.

THE 16PF IN ACTION

Figure 2 is my own 16PF profile reproduced on the standard 16PF profile form. You can see from the profile that I have some interesting strengths and weaknesses. However, as interesting as the profile might be, it only represents a small part of the story. To interpret the profile in more detail the 16PF second order factors are used. These second order factors which have been developed over a number of years are mainly based on detailed research by academics into specific areas of interest. The second order factors are all arrived at using equations based on the original profile scores.

To illustrate how the second order factors are used I have had my 16PF primary trait scores run through an IPAT-approved 16PF computer support program called The Personal Career Development Profile (PCDP). The program uses the 16PF results to generate a detailed eight-page report for expert interpretation.

The report provides detailed information on the following:

(1) Problem-solving patterns
(2) Patterns for coping with stressful conditions
(3) Patterns of interpersonal interaction
(4) Organisational role and work-setting patterns
(5) Patterns for career activity interests
(6) Personal career life-style effectiveness considerations

It ends with occupational scores comparisons and considerations for counselling and feedback. Section (6) of the report 'Personal-Career Life-style Effectiveness Considerations' is reproduced as Figure 3. Anybody who knows me well will confirm the accuracy of the comments made.

It is clear from the headings used in the PCDP report that the information generated and then interpreted would be very beneficial in designing a management development schedule for any individual manager.

A number of other people have developed aids to using the 16PF and I would like to refer to two of these.

KRUG'S 16PF PROFILE PATTERNS

In 1981 Sam Krug, one of the leading psychologists in the world working on the 16PF, published a book on interpreting 16PF profiles. The book contains 81 composite profiles. Krug uses the four main second order factors of the 16PF to develop an easy method of classifying some 17,000 possible 16PF profile patterns. He has in fact condensed the 17,000 possible profile patterns to 81 by finding the modal

Meaning of score on left	Standard Ten Score (STEN) →Average← 1 2 3 4 5 6 7 8 9 10	Meaning of score on right
Cool, reserved, impersonal, detached, formal, aloof	A (7)	Warm, outgoing, kindly, easy-going, participating, likes people
Concrete-thinking, less intelligent	B (10)	Abstract-thinking, more intelligent, bright
Affected by feelings, emotionally less stable, easily annoyed	C (5)	Emotionally stable, mature, faces reality, calm
Submissive, humble, mild, easily led, accommodating	E (9)	Dominant, assertive, aggressive, stubborn, competitive, bossy
Sober, restrained, prudent, taciturn, serious	F (8)	Enthusiastic, impulsive, heedless, expressive, cheerful
Expedient, disregards rules, self-indulgent	G (4)	Conscientious, persistent, moralistic, staid, rule-bound
Shy, threat-sensitive, timid, hesitant, intimidated	H (8)	Bold, venturesome, uninhibited, can take stress
Tough-minded, self-reliant, no-nonsense, rough, realistic	I (6)	Tender-minded, sensitive, over-protected, intuitive, refined
Trusting, accepting conditions, easy to get on with	L (4)	Suspicious, hard to fool, distrustful, sceptical
Practical, concerned with 'down to earth' issues, steady	M (6)	Imaginative, absent-minded, absorbed in thought, impractical
Forthright, unpretentious, open, genuine, artless	N (3)	Shrewd, polished, socially aware, diplomatic, calculating
Self-assured, secure, feels free of guilt, untroubled, self-satisfied	O (3)	Apprehensive, self-blaming, guilt-prone, insecure, worrying
Conservative, respecting traditional ideas	Q_1 (9)	Experimenting, liberal, critical, open to change
Group-oriented, a 'joiner' and sound follower, listens to others	Q_2 (6)	Self-sufficient, resourceful, prefers own decisions
Undisciplined self-conflict, lax, careless of social rules	Q_3 (5)	Controlled, self-respecting, socially precise, compulsive
Relaxed, tranquil, composed, has low drive, unfrustrated	Q_4 (7)	Tense, frustrated, overwrought, has high drive

A sten of	1	2	3	4	5	6	7	8	9	10	is obtained
by about	2.3%	4.4%	9.2%	15.0%	19.1%	19.1%	15.0%	9.2%	4.4%	2.3%	of adults

FIG. 2. STANDARD 16PF PROFILE.

Mr. Watts' life style is typical of people who value self-directedness and independence. He generally strives to achieve control of and freedom of choice in his personal life and work-related situations. He shows a marked preference for activities and work which involves meeting and interacting with people. He generally strives to help people and usually gets a great deal of satisfaction from doing things for others. He generally gains much satisfaction when he is in a position of leadership and is able to direct the actions of others. Mr. Watts performs well and experiences most satisfaction when he is assigned to a work situation which provides him a lot of leeway, involves a variety of different activity so he can be as innovative as possible, and is somewhat loose in structure. If the structure of the job allows, working conditions might be changed for him to allow enough freedom from group pressures so that Mr. Watts can go his own way in the job.

In terms of Mr. Watts' needs for performance effectiveness and self-growth, he could be urged to guard against: (*) his tendency, at times, to act with so much eagerness, energy and optimism that he may overlook important details; fail to prepare himself enough for what he undertakes; or sufficiently anticipate consequences of what he does; (*) viewing important matters too subjectively, that is, permitting his feeling sensitivity to colour his judgements in situations that could be best resolved with rational, cool-headedness; (*) the tendency to make spur of the moment decisions, rather than preparing himself enough before making decisions and taking action or giving thoughtful consideration of possible consequences of such actions; (*) tendencies to become overly impatient, or demanding and excitable, when trying to get others to accept what he wants done, or when confronted with what he may view as possible roadblocks to doing things valued by him as being very important; (*) being overly confident about his ability to handle almost any problems or situations that come up when more accurate thinking and more realistic planning may be required to accomplish what he most desires to do; (*) being in such a hurry to get things done that he does not see how others may feel about things that are important to them; (*) dealing with others in a way which may make people feel rejected or ignored, especially if they think differently than he does about the issues at hand; (*) trying so hard at times to get others to do things that he thinks are important that perhaps he forgets to remember the needs of others; (*) expecting others to rely on themselves in getting jobs done without controlling, following up and giving guidelines to them to make sure others do a good job; (*) being so natural and forthright when relating with others that the need to be critically insightful and/or politically and socially astute are overlooked or not valued sufficiently; (*) pressing so hard in work-related and other personal situations that opportunities to relax are given less than needed attention; and (*) taking on activities or assignments which involve ordinary, routine tasks without much creative thought or tasks which may not fully challenge Mr. Watts intelligence or curiosity.

In conclusion, Mr. Watts seems to place importance on making an honest and sincere impression when he presents himself to others. He is usually very happy and willing to simply be himself in most situations.

FIG. 3. A PERSONAL CAREER DEVELOPMENT PROFILE.

score on each factor. Using Krug's book the method is as follows:

To access a profile it is necessary to score the first four second order factors thus:

below 4.0   = 1
between 4.0 and 7.0 = 2
over 7.0   = 3

Using the second-order factors from my 16PF the results are:

Extroversion 9.6   = 3
Anxiety 4.3   = 2
Tough poise 7.4   = 3
Independence 10.0   = 3

From this result profile pattern 3–2–3–3 in Krug's book can be accessed to gain a more detailed understanding of 16PF results.

Krug's book is a good 'quick and dirty' way of looking at a manager's profile, but it is limited. If you are going to use the 16PF as a serious management development tool, you will need access to someone who can give you a detailed analysis of a profile. I will return to this point later.

WALTER'S CAREER THEME SCORES

The Personal-Career Development Profile (PCDP) also generates a list of career theme scores. These scores are the result of work by Walter in 1979 to measure Holland's six broad personality orientations which Holland theorised could be found in the world of work. Figure 4 represents a simple set of definitions for these; it is laid out so that you can reproduce it for your managers.

For an example of how the career themes work in practice the scores from my 16PF can be used:

Analytic–investigative (scientific)   7.7
Creative–self-expressive   10.0
Mechanical–operative   4.3
Nurturing–altruistic   8.8
Procedural–systematic   5.7
Venturous–influential   9.7

It is possible to conclude from these scores that I have the right characteristics for a managerial position involving high people-contact, the generation of new ideas and problem-solving. If however, the management position involves lots of detailed technical application and paperwork, I would be less fitted for the position and would probably not perform these tasks well. I can confirm to you that this is very true.

In general I find the Walter career-theme scores both very accurate

16PF Career theme	Preferences	Corresponding Holland theme
Analytic–scientific *****	Activities involving problem-solving and analytic skills	Investigative
Creative–self-expressive ***	Activities involving innovation and the production of new concepts	Artistic
Mechanical–operative *	Activities involving machines & tools etc	Realistic
Nurturing–altruistic ****	Activities involving other people	Social
Procedural–systematic **	Activities involving clerical skills	Conventional
Venturous–influential *****	Activities involving persuasive skills and the control of others	Enterprising

Note: Asterisks indicate my estimation of the weight of each theme in relation to the abilities and skills needed for management.

FIG. 4. WALTER'S CAREER THEME SCORES.

and very useful. Now let's consider how they might work in your organisation.

I hope by now that we are agreed that you need managers who have above average:

(a) analytical and investigative abilities and skills;
(b) creative abilities and skills;
(c) people-handling ability and skills.

If, by using the 16PF Walter career-theme scores, you can identify in your managers personality characteristics and behavioural tendencies that point to the possession of those skills and abilities, then you have made a big step forward in planning their further development. If, however, by using the 16PF you identify that some of your managers score below average in these areas then you have pinpointed problem managers who require more basic management development. It's really a case of 'Heads I win, tails you lose'; you need this management development book either way.

Krug's composite profiles and Walter's career themes are just two examples of ways of developing the information generated by the 16PF profiles. In Chapter Four I will show how the Belbin factors which can also be generated from the 16PF can be used in the development of your management team.

GETTING TO GRIPS WITH THE 16PF

The 16PF has many other uses as a management development tool and you may wish to consider these. To find out more about the 16PF, how to use and generally administer it, you have three options:

(1) Become qualified to use it yourself. If you have the right academic and job background you can become qualified by attending a 16PF course. These courses last about seven days and are followed by periods of supervised probation. Depending on your qualifications and background you may also first have to become qualified to administer aptitude-type tests and assessments. Again the aptitude-related courses last about seven days with periods of supervised probation.

(2) Qualify one of your staff to use it. Most personnel and training people like to get this qualification.

(3) Work with a professional organisation which offers a 16PF service.

If you live in the UK there are a number of reputable organisations who provide 16PF materials and training to suitably qualified people.

NFER-Nelson is the publisher, distributor and exclusive agent for the sale and distribution of 16PF materials in the UK. They are responsible for co-ordinating and supervising computerised services in their territory. You should be careful not to use or purchase any unauthorised

16PF computer programs as these infringe international copyright laws.

The Independent Assessment and Research Centre, Principal Dr Ken Miller, is the exclusive provider of the Personal-Career Development Profile (PCDP) in the UK.

The Test Agency, which is a small, highly professional organisation run by Phylis and David Morgan, provides approved training for the 16PF and a number of other useful assessments.

The appendix gives addresses for all these organisations.

CHAPTER SUMMARY: THE 'IDEAL MANAGER PROFILE'

(1) As a result of working through this chapter, you and your managers should now be able to define clearly all the qualities needed to be an effective manager in your organisation.

(2) As a result of your use of the assessment processes in this chapter, you now know how to assess both your present and future managers—that is, in such a way as to maximise your understanding of their characteristics, behavioural tendencies, abilities and skills.

These two progress stages are highly significant and should alter for ever the way management is considered in your organisation.

Before you move onto Chapter 3, I would like to present you with that elusive 'ideal manager profile'. Figure 5 represents the collective views of many 16PF users, gathered over a number of years, of an 'ideal manager's profile'. The profile has been developed along lines similar to those used by Krug for his set of profile patterns. Two of Krug's patterns are covered: 3133 and 3132. The black dots represent the results that would be used to generate the exact second-order factors. Section (4) of a PCDP report, 'Organisational Role and Work-setting Patterns', generated from the second-order factors, is reproduced as Figure 6.

I hope you find the profile interesting; keep it by you when you are considering any assessment of a 16PF, but remember never to stop using your own judgement. After all, judgement is a management skill.

Don't forget you can obtain extra copies of MAC and MATE, complete with computer report writing and database support systems, via the follow-up service described in the appendix.

Meaning of score on left	Standard Ten Score (STEN) →Average←	Meaning of score on right
1 2 3 4 5 6 7 8 9 10		
Cool, reserved, impersonal, detached, formal, aloof	A (profile band ~7–9)	Warm, outgoing, kindly, easy-going, participating, likes people
Concrete-thinking, less intelligent	B (profile band ~8–10)	Abstract-thinking, more intelligent, bright
Affected by feelings, emotionally less stable, easily annoyed	C (profile band ~5–10)	Emotionally stable, mature, faces reality, calm
Submissive, humble, mild, easily led, accommodating	E (profile band ~7–9)	Dominant, assertive, aggressive, stubborn, competitive, bossy
Sober, restrained, prudent, taciturn, serious	F (profile band ~6–9)	Enthusiastic, impulsive, heedless, expressive, cheerful
Expedient, disregards rules, self-indulgent	G (profile band ~4–8)	Conscientious, persistent, moralistic, staid, rule-bound
Shy, threat-sensitive, timid, hesitant, intimidated	H (profile band ~7–10)	Bold, venturesome, uninhibited, can take stress
Tough-minded, self-reliant, no-nonsense, rough, realistic	I (profile band ~3–6)	Tender-minded, sensitive, over-protected, intuitive, refined
Trusting, accepting conditions, easy to get on with	L (profile band ~3–5)	Suspicious, hard to fool, distrustful, sceptical
Practical, concerned with 'down to earth' issues, steady	M (profile band ~3–8)	Imaginative, absent-minded, absorbed in thought, impractical
Forthright, unpretentious, open, genuine, artless	N (profile band ~4–7)	Shrewd, polished, socially aware, diplomatic, calculating
Self-assured, secure, feels free of guilt, untroubled, self-satisfied	O (profile band ~1–3)	Apprehensive, self-blaming, guilt-prone, insecure, worrying
Conservative, respecting traditional ideas	Q₁ (profile band ~3–8)	Experimenting, liberal, critical, open to change
Group-oriented, a 'joiner' and sound follower, listens to others	Q₂ (profile band ~4–7)	Self-sufficient, resourceful, prefers own decisions
Undisciplined self-conflict, lax, careless of social rules	Q₃ (profile band ~6–8)	Controlled, self-respecting, socially precise, compulsive
Relaxed, tranquil, composed, has low drive, unfrustrated	Q₄ (profile band ~4–6)	Tense, frustrated, overwrought, has high drive

A sten of	1	2	3	4	5	6	7	8	9	10	is obtained
by about	2.3%	4.4%	9.2%	15.0%	19.1%	19.1%	15.0%	9.2%	4.4%	2.3%	of adults

FIG. 5. THE 'IDEAL MANAGER' PROFILE.

Mr. Manager tends to experience considerable satisfaction when he is given the chance to be in a position of leadership in most organisational settings. He likes to be in charge of others, particularly a group of friends or co-workers. He usually feels comfortable in situations which require him to provide direction over others. His group members, too, are likely to respond favourably to his leadership patterns. Mr. Manager generally attempts to influence others by directing, persuading and challenging them to get things done. He seems to truly enjoy talking and interacting with people to get them to agree with his points of view when it's important to him. If he were to take on a leadership role with others, he would probably strive to administer duties by focusing attention on the conditions which foster or hinder the performance of subordinates rather than on personnel problems which may be present. Being more solution-seeking than blame oriented, he strives to remove personality and power struggles from the work situation. Mr. Manager generally prefers to build feelings of mutual respect and interdependence among people. He usually likes to share with others whatever power may be necessary to accomplish assignments. He appears to value objective working relationships between superiors and subordinates. Mr. Manager appears to want to be a source of objective criticism and feedback to others. He also likes to be part of work settings where responsibility, power and accountability are shared with others.

Mr. Manager is likely to feel most at home when working in relaxed and flexible settings that are not boring or routine in nature. If some structure would be necessary, he likes to design it himself rather than having someone else impose it on him. He has a strong sense of duty and responsibility. He also has fairly strong beliefs as to what is right and wrong in most situations. He generally, therefore, holds to rather strict standards at times so others will think well of him. He should enjoy and do a good job on troubleshooting-type assignments in which he has chances to tackle and solve difficult problems. Mr. Manager appears to be able to do quite a few things well and probably does well in his efforts to use his experience in solving old and new problems in jobs. He seems quite appreciative of time-tested values and ways of doing things.

FIG. 6. A PERSONAL CAREER DEVELOPMENT PROFILE.

3

MEASURING MANAGERIAL PERFORMANCE

Once you can pinpoint the 'hands on' management activities of each manager in your team you will be able to jointly agree performance standards for the various activities.

During the course of this chapter each manager will be asked to define the four or five key segments of their job: that is, the managerial activities they must perform well to be regarded as effective. Together you and each manager will then discuss and agree performance standards for these segments. A 'hands on' performance sheet for structuring and monitoring the key segments and standards will be presented for you to reproduce. Examples of completed sheets, with background information to the segment, will also be provided for guidance. Finally you will be asked to agree, with each manager, dates for reviewing the agreed segments and performance standards to ensure they remain relevant.

At the end of this chapter both you and each member of your management team will have a complete and on-going flexible system for monitoring performance. You will have learnt a lot about the background to each key segment and you will have achieved the two central objectives in the creation of the 'hands on' manager:

▶ *The definition of each manager's key job segments with performance standards for each.*

▶ *The setting up of the 'hands on' managerial performance monitoring system.*

USING MANAGERS FOR MANAGING

Let's start this chapter with a question. Why were your managers hired? Take a few minutes to write down the answer.

DISCOVERY EXERCISE

Listing reasons for hiring managers.   *Allow 5 minutes.*

Look closely at your answer. It is my guess that you have probably made statements along the following lines.

They were hired:

- To solve a particular delegation or control problem arising from expansion.
- To take charge of a situation that needed new leadership.
- To start up a new project.
- To relieve the pressure of work experienced by another manager.
- To deal with a poor motivation problem and stimulate better personnel performance.

All answers that sound fine, but if you think a bit harder all these descriptions are difficult to quantify and the performance of them, as described, even more difficult to measure.

What I am quite sure you didn't state is:

- Making the tea.
- Cleaning the office.
- Filing last week's correspondence.
- Filling in staff expenses claims.
- Debating the allocation of car parking spaces.
- Deciding the staff canteen menu.
- Designing the layout of your organisation's reception area.
- Checking that all the office doors are locked last thing at night.

Although these activities sound ridiculous they are all actual examples written down by managers from major organisations in answer to the question 'What do *you* do?' They are also activities that are easy both to quantify and to measure. Now stop and ask yourself what your own managers might put down. Write down your thoughts.

DISCOVERY EXERCISE

What do your managers do?   *Allow 5 minutes.*

I have asked you to make these comparisons because both sets of activities will tend to be very important to the daily life of your organisation. Agreeing the difference between the two is even more important.

This leads us to the first lesson of this chapter.

▶ *There is a major difference between activities that ensure the smooth running of your organisation and the activities that direct your organisation towards the achievement of its objectives.*

Your managers were hired to manage parts of your organisation so that the organisation as a whole can achieve its objectives. This means you want your managers to spend their time, applied energy and effort on real management activities not just keeping things happy and moving along. In fact some of the activities you might require your managers to undertake could cause real upsets in the day-to-day routines of your people.

▶ *Never forget your managers are there to make positive things happen.*

'Hands on' managers will be skilled both at making positive things happen and at the same time retaining the confidence of their team. These managers will only use assertiveness in a positive way and their people will respect them for their drive and determination to help the organisation to win.

The positive attitude of your managers will ensure that your organisation contains active happy people who expect their managers to take them forward and keep the organisation strong. They expect their managers to present them with challenges and changes, not as reactions to events but to shape events. Most of all the people in such an organisation want to share in the organisation's success and they know this means their managers will ask a lot of them.

THE KEY SEGMENTS OF EACH MANAGER'S JOB

If you have worked your way through Chapters One and Two, your managers know what they are currently doing, how much time they are spending doing it and their strengths and weaknesses in relation to their role in your organisation. A positive attitude has therefore already been established. The exercises in Chapters One and Two have also started your managers on the process of relating their work to the 'hands on' management activities. They should now be ready to define their own activities in detail and agree with you a performance standard for each.

In a winning organisation (the type of organisation you are creating) all managerial positions have key segments, usually four or five. These are the vital areas of responsibility which, if not handled efficiently, will result in your managers' performance being considered unsatisfactory and your organisation's effectiveness being reduced.

An easy way for your managers to start identifying the key segments of their jobs is to use the core 'hands on' management activities as a quick reference. They need to look at the activity they are trying to define and ensure it fits under one of the five headings. If it doesn't, the chances are it is not a truly managerial activity. Once the activities have all been checked against the 'core' activities, the defining process can begin.

To help your managers with writing down their key segments I have provided specific examples, with performance standards, for each of the core management activities. You might also like to use the overhead transparencies you prepared for the core 'hands on' activities for Chapter One to support your discussions.

The first two examples cover *the 'core' management activity of the top team supporter.* You will recall that this activity is concerned with:

▶ *Assisting senior management with budgets, meeting targets and achieving objectives:*

Example one is taken from the performance sheet of a marketing manager and example two is taken from the performance sheet of an R and D manager. Both examples cover the planning and budgeting process required, in some form or other, by most organisations.

When looking at the two examples you should consider the following points relating to the planning and budgeting process.
(1) The planning and budgeting process is vital to ensuring your organisation remains pro-active in relation to its operating environment. Remember:

▶ *Organisations that can only react to situations usually get lots of nasty surprises.*

(2) Many managers consider the organisation planning and budgeting process an interruption of their work rather than the foundation necessary for its success. Remember:

▶ *Planning for the future is a cornerstone activity of the 'hands on' manager.*

(3) The simple way to overcome any managerial antipathy towards planning and budgeting is not to *impose* budgets, targets and objectives on your managers; remember:

▶ *Managers who have the last word on their budgets, targets and objectives usually achieve them.*

(4) The time spent on planning and budgeting should not be considered extra to normal duties. Allocate plenty of time for the process; it is managerial time well spent. Remember:

▶ *Planning and budgeting is like training for a big sporting event; the team that has prepared best always has the greatest chance of winning.*

(5) Do not make the planning and budgeting process unnecessarily complicated. Everyone who is required to implement your plans and budgets should be able to involve themselves without difficulty. Remember:

▶ *The more involvement you allow, the more positive commitment you create. Commitment is what makes plans work, not complex procedures.*

THE MARKETING MANAGER

The first *top team supporter* example concerns a marketing manager. Marketing is the starting function of most commercial organisations, even if they don't have a marketing department. Remember:
NOTHING STARTS WITHOUT A SALE.

In recent years marketing activities have become very sophisticated and data-dependent. In the past products were launched because somebody believed in them; today, unless research data supports a launch, it does not happen. This often results in the spending of lots of money by a team of specialists all of whom are considered to be essential support for the marketing manager. I am afraid I remain a supporter of 'feel' and like to work with marketing managers who still use their intuition as well as data to make key marketing decisions.

Whether you have a marketing manager who works just by numbers or by judgement and data, marketing decisions must reflect the reality of the world in which your organisation operates. The marketing budget and plan affects all the other activities of your organisation. Remember:

▶ *A wrong sales forecast by the marketing department can never be put right by the production, finance or personnel departments.*

Because marketing is mainly external to the organisation activity and spends big money, the pressure is always on for tangible results. The marketing manager's job segments should be designed to ensure that the temptation to go for short-term success to appease the rest of the management team is avoided. There is no substitute for proper market appraisal, followed by considered marketing actions.

DEVELOPMENT GUIDE 10

'Core' Management Activity: Top Team Supporter

EXAMPLE 1 THE MARKETING MANAGER

JOB SEGMENT DESCRIPTION

To prepare every July for presentation to the senior management team the marketing plan and budget for the coming year. This plan and budget should detail:

(1) A review of the previous year with a situation report covering:
(a) Products and services.
(b) Markets—sizes and trends.
(c) Competition—product, price, quality, and distribution comparisons.

(2) A statement of goals and strategy expressed in:
(a) Return on capital employed.
(b) Percentage market share.
(c) Net sales revenue.

(3) A plan of action with timetable, detailing who does what and when, for:
(a) Products and services, features and development.
(b) Pricing.
(c) Field and telephone sales.
(d) Sales promotion and public relations.
(e) Advertising and sponsorships.
(f) Exhibitions.
(g) Market research.

You can see from this example that all the activities under the control of this manager are covered. This manager has to consider each activity when preparing the plan and budget. The tasks cannot be completed properly without the manager being pro-active:

- Market conditions have to be explored.
- Key staff have to be consulted and their tasks described.
- Targets have to be expressed in a quantified way.

This manager cannot afford to be anything but 'hands on'. Setting the performance standard for this key segment is now an easy task.

JOB SEGMENT PERFORMANCE STANDARD

Performance will be considered satisfactory if:

(1) The plan and budget meet the requirements of and fully contribute to the corporate objectives of the organisation.
(2) The plan and budget is approved by the senior management team by the end of August each year.

Note: The marketing plan and budget must be submitted and approved ahead of all other budgets and plans. The marketing manager therefore has a responsibility to ensure that all other managers have full access to the plans and targets figures as soon as they are approved.

It is also important to keep the marketing manager's feet on the ground. Remember:

▶ *If the marketing department's latest research technique is too complicated to explain, take it out of the budget.*

'Hands on' marketing managers think 'total market' and will want to ensure that all the activities under the marketing umbrella are co-ordinated. They know that sales is not a 'Cinderella activity' and that customers believe in people not just adverts. They know that research data is not written on tablets of stone. They know that successful advertising requires a tight advertising brief and that competitors are not always perfect. *Their* budgets and plans will reflect *their* total market approach.

Simple isn't it? This manager is not being overtly controlled but now knows exactly what standards have to be met and when they have to be met. Remember in a winning organisation all managers contribute to the development of the organisation's objectives and advise senior management on long-term objectives and plans. Also, in a winning organisation, all managers will seek to co-operate with each other in the development of each other's plans and budgets. Successful managers realise how dependent they are on each other for that success.

THE R AND D MANAGER

The next *top team supporter* example concerns a research and development manager. Research and development people often consider themselves to be outside the day-to-day activities of the organisation. Many organistions don't in fact closely examine the performance of R and D people. If you have an R and D facility then beware of falling into the same trap as Rolls-Royce did in 1970; that is, allowing R and D unlimited funds based on false expectations. Remember:

STANDARDS ARE FOR EVERYBODY.

In a winning organisation R and D people will expect to be accountable for their performance; they will understand how vital their activities are to the organisation's long-term success.

By way of an example, let me tell you about the last R and D department in an organisation I looked at. This organisation was spending £4 million a year on various developments and projects; this represented 30% of the organisation's turnover. When discussing performance with its management I was amazed to find that none of these managers considered it necessary to meet targets related to corporate objectives. Targets in fact were regarded as just loose guidelines not to be taken too seriously. A closer inspection of their actual performance revealed that

DEVELOPMENT GUIDE 11

'Core' Management Activity: Top Team Supporter

EXAMPLE 2 THE R AND D MANAGER

JOB SEGMENT DESCRIPTION

To prepare by January, for presentation to the senior management team, the research and development plan and budget for the coming financial year.

Also to prepare for presentation at the same time a five year expenditure plan for new product concepts (blue skies money).

These plans and budgets to detail:

(1) The progress and future programme for all products under development or being researched.
(2) The costs to date and projected costs for all products under development or being researched with an expenditure which is likely to exceed £25,000.
(3) A timetable for the handover of projects or products to engineering for preparation for application testing or manufacture.
(4) Recommendations for capital expenditure on new research and development related equipment.
(5) Recommendations for long term specialised staffing.

 The argument R and D people put forward against working to plans, budgets and timetables is that such activities stifle creativity and innovation. The 'hands on' performance sheet presented deals square and fair with that argument. This manager is able to spend money on 'blue skies' projects, ensure he has the specialised skilled staff he needs, free small projects of cost controls and plan for new equipment. At the same time he is in control of the team he leads as this segment is designed to ensure he automatically monitors all the projects his team are working on. The organisation is also able to maintain a pro-active mode because they know when products and projects will be leaving R and D. Writing the performance standard for this segment is straightforward.
 The performance standard is very similar to the one for the marketing manager. Once again, this manager knows exactly what is expected of him. The key point in both examples is the stress on the need to co-operate with other managers.

JOB SEGMENT PERFORMANCE STANDARDS

Performance will be considered satisfactory if:

(1) The submitted plan and budget meets the corporate objectives of the organisation.
(2) The plan and budget is approved by the senior management team by the end of October each year.

Note: The research and development plan will contain timetables for existing developments and new products. These timetables affect the plans and budgets of other managers. The R and D manager has a responsibility to ensure all other managers have access to these timetables by the end of July each year.

no new products had been produced from R and D activities in eight years and the organisation had fallen well behind its competitors as a result. These managers were not bad people but they had developed habits that had made them very bad managers. One even considered attending between 18 and 24 meetings a week was managerial. To remain competitive this organisation had to buy in new product lines. It had allowed its managers to become 'hands off' and had to pay a high price as a result.

THE FINANCIAL MANAGER

The next example covers *the 'core' management activity* of the *buck stops captain*. You will recall that this activity is concerned with:

 Organising, allocating and controlling the work and performance of the manager's own team.

The example is taken from the performance sheet of a financial manager. It focuses on relations; that is, the relationships that need to be established between members of a work team for successful collective task completion and the relationships that need to exist between different departmental teams.

When looking at the example you should consider the following points related to the organising, work allocation and control process.

(1) Many managers do not fully appreciate the benefits of ensuring that everybody knows what is expected of them and how their role relates to the work of other members of the team. This leads, all too often, to negative rather than positive synergy. Managers who allow this situation to arise will find themselves constantly trying to fill the gaps between the tasks of different team members. Remember:

 Creating positive synergy through team work is a cornerstone activity of the 'hands on' manager.

(2) In my experience there are four basic reasons why tasks don't get completed on time, in the right way, or within their original budget. They are:

(a) *Too many people have a part of the task to do.*

(b) *No one individual has overall responsibility for seeing the task is completed.*

(c) *How the task is to be carried out has not been clearly defined and confidently agreed.*

DEVELOPMENT GUIDE 12

'Core' Management Activity: Buck Stops Captain

EXAMPLE 3 THE FINANCIAL MANAGER

JOB SEGMENT DESCRIPTION

(1) To agree with each member of the accounting and finance team their key tasks, performance standards and authority for the next 12 months, by:

(a) One-to-one no status interview. At the interview to encourage the team member to define their job in their own terms, discuss the authority they need and then jointly agree performance standards.

The standards agreed at these annual interviews will be monitored every two months at informal one-to-one interviews. These interviews are to encourage the team member to discuss their actual performance and progress against the agreed standards and make adjustments where necessary.

(2) To agree and re-define every month the work relationships between members of the accounting and finance team and to discuss and agree the team's work relationships with other departments, by:

(a) Leading discussions between team members on existing task allocation and how they intend to integrate and absorb new tasks, and leading discussions on how to meet the routine and special needs of other departments arising from the organisation's changing operations.

JOB SEGMENT PERFORMANCE STANDARD

Performance will be considered satisfactory if:

(1) One-to-one key tasks interviews are held every 12 months with all staff. These interviews are to be spaced out through the year to avoid the 'annual appraisal syndrome'.
(2) The tasks and standards agreed at the 12–monthly interviews are recorded and reviewed bi-monthly at one-to-one interviews.
(3) Team-work relationship meetings are to be held monthly to agree, and redefine if necessary, inter-team tasks and the provision of support to other departments.

By agreeing to these standards this manager:

(1) Avoids overt interference with the day-to-day work of the team, but is totally in the picture as to what each member of the team and the team as a whole is doing.
(2) Is in a position to discuss, with confidence, the team's provision of support with all the other managers who might require it.

(d) The abilities of the individuals required to complete the task do not match those required by the task.

I am sure you have often heard football team managers use (d) as an excuse for their team's poor performance. This is rarely either fair or true. A team of very ordinary individuals, if organised well, will nearly always beat a team of disorganised but talented individuals. The difference is in the way a team is managed.

'Hands on' managers will know all there is to know about the skills and limitations of their team members. They will always seek to stretch them and develop them to their maximum capability. They will carefully delegate tasks and never dump work on those for whom they are responsible. All too often I have witnessed managers throwing people in at the deep end and then taking the credit when the same people manage to swim. Skilled managers always create a demanding but secure environment for their people to grow in. In the long term they know that their people will achieve a lot more and will make their task of managing a lot easier if they adopt this approach.

The financial and accounting function always has a lot of control over what happens in other areas of the organisation. It is often the area which the other departments love to hate. For their part accounting and finance people often tend to promote the idea that they would prefer an organisation without other people or customers.

Unless your organisation is one in which the prime activity is making money with money then your finance and accounting department is a support department and needs to be organised and controlled so that it acts in a supportive way. The people who work in this area need to be developed so they have a clear understanding of how they are required to support other departments. They also need to develop an appreciation of the importance of the work of other people in the organisation generally. These are all activities that must be reflected in the finance manager's key job segments.

The finance and accounts department is also a major generator of important information for the organisation. As information can make, or the lack of it break, an organisation, remember:

▶ *To be of value information must be correct, simply presented and quickly delivered to those who need to use or have knowledge of it.*

In a winning organisation the jobs of finance and accounts people will have built into them the relationships they must have and foster with the rest of the organisation. 'Hands on' finance managers will structure their department so that it is accessible to other managers and specialist people who need figures. They will see that information is supplied in a user-friendly format and laid out so that the recipients can make best use of it. They will ensure their team is always seeking to develop systems that respond quickly to current needs and remove the mysteries of figures. They recognise:

THE IMPORTANCE OF A TOTAL ORGANISATION APPROACH.

At first glance the finance manager's job seems to comprise more than one segment; a closer inspection reveals that the activities are, in fact, integrated. The objective is to ensure the manager manages the team members by getting them to do the work in their own way, while at the same time serving the organisation's needs.

You will see from this *buck stops captain* example that the manager will have a clear picture of both the collective work of the team and the individual contribution of each member. The importance of this segment does not end there: this segment is written so it remains dynamic. 'Hands on' managers have to keep their team stretched by regularly reviewing their capability and adjusting (in the main raising) their performance standards. At the same time they need to look outwards to check that the team is supporting the organisation as it should. Once again, regular time is set aside for manager and team to review how they support the rest of the organisation.

In accepting responsibility for the team's performance the *buck stops captain* is not bravely protecting them from difficulties and challenges. Leadership based on a complete knowledge of the team's capability, with the team's full co-operation and agreed commitment allows the manager freely to accept and agree new challenges on the team's behalf. Such managers can confidently accept responsibility for all of the team's actions because they agreed them.

MOTIVATED BEHAVIOUR

The next example covers *the 'core' management activity of the own-team coach*. You will recall that this activity is concerned with

MOTIVATING, MOULDING AND MONITORING THE PERFORMANCE OF EACH MEMBER OF THE TEAM.

The example is taken from the performance sheet of a Personnel Manager. The example covers the department's individual staff training and development process. Of course all managers should be concerned with the development of their staff but the activity is particularly poignant in the department which is concerned with human resources. This is, after all, the department all the other managers look to, or should look to, for advice on training and development.

At first this activity appears to be similar to the *buck stops captain* activity. There are of course similarities: the difference lies in their focus. *The buck stops captain* activity focuses on relationships while the *own team coach* activity focuses on maintaining motivation and the development of ability.

As well as establishing an environment in which people clearly know what is expected of them, the 'hands on' manager must also develop the abilities of team members so that they match the changing demands faced by the organisation. This of course pays dividends to the organisation as the more people are capable of doing, the more versatile and useful they become. However a word of warning here; remember:

▶ *The more people can do, the more they will want to do.*

When you develop and train people make sure you are in a position to let them use their new skills otherwise you may find them working against you. Remember:

▶ *Motivated behaviour is a product of ability and opportunity.*

If you increase people's ability and then deprive them of the opportunity to use it they are likely to use it against you.

Human motivation is a complex issue. The first thing to remember is that it changes constantly, in some cases from hour to hour. The one common factor in people's motivation is money.

Despite all the books on motivation that say otherwise, money plays the biggest part in the performance of people and is the one vehicle that can help satisfy the widest range of individual needs. To make it work as a motivator money requires the development of an association between the money, the specific individual need and the performance. This is no easy task as managers who only use money to solve motivation problems often find to their cost. The answer is not to use money as a threat. Most people need to feel that their income is secure and not a constantly re-negotiable variable. There are of course those individuals who thrive in commission-only situations but they are exceptions and should be treated as such. In most organisations it is important to remember:

▶ *Money enables people to attend. Consideration, responsibility and development opportunies enable people to contribute.*

If you use money wisely, then it works as a motivator for you all on its own and lets you get on with the more important task of getting the best out of people.

It is also very important to remember that people have different ability levels which should always be matched to their job.

For example, you should never recruit people whose ability already exceeds the best work you can offer them. They will always do the work badly and resent you for giving it to them. You should never be over-impressed with educational qualifications (remember they don't major on life skills at schools and colleges). Always pick people who can demonstrate an aptitude for the work and will like doing it. By all means develop people for a job or into a job but always upwards never downwards. This is an important concept and by way of illustration I would like to quote two actual examples.

(1) *DEPARTMENT OF HEALTH AND SOCIAL SECURITY* At the start of the UK rise in unemployment I was invited to look at a problem of high staff turnover in an unemployment benefits office. The Department of Health and Social Security had decided to raise the standard of entry requirements for counter service to two GCE 'A' levels. Previously, this work was often handled by mature women returning to work after bringing up a family. These women had an aptitude for the work, they understood the clients' problems and were generally able to deal with the difficult situations that constantly arose. But they lacked the necessary two A levels. Slowly they were replaced by recent school leavers looking for employment opportunities themselves. The clients at this particular office were, in the main either Irish, West Indian or Pakistani ex-construction or factory workers with families to support. No amount of induction training could prepare the recent school leavers for the conditions they were to encounter doing this work: they were completely out of their depth. The results were very predictable and sad for both the clients and the staff. The lesson is very clear: always match aptitude to task.

(2) *BREWERY* By contrast I used to visit a brewery regularly to show trainee managers how to manage technology. This brewery was the best example of automation I have ever seen. The production output amounted to 50 million gallons of lager a year from a total staff of just over two hundred people.

The brewery had no industrial relations problems and had a very low staff turnover. When I discussed this happy state of affairs with the personnel manager I found that it has not materialised by accident. The company recognised that the work that they could offer was, in general, boring and solitary. It was however essential that it was done well. They spent a great deal of time and effort picking people who could spend long hours looking at dials and automated production lines to ensure all was well. They paid the people very high wages and employed more people than they needed to allow for regular breaks in work to reduce boredom.

They provided a very active social atmosphere as further compensation and ensured that the workers were able to make a direct association between their contribution and the company's success. Now I am not making a case for boring work or reducing education, but I am recommending 'horses for courses'.

Developing Motivated Behaviour

How should the 'hands on' manager develop people and ensure that they are motivated to help the organisation achieve its objectives?

The process of generating motivated behaviour and developing people into their roles has three parts.

(1) First, it is necessary to have a clear understanding of what has to be achieved. This should have already been done via the *buck stops captain* activity.

(2) Second, it is necessary to know what each member of the team is capable of. This can be achieved by getting to know more about them and building up a picture of them beyond their immediate work role. Discuss with them their ambitions and what they enjoy about their work. Find out about their interests and hobbies.

Look at their employment track record. Ask them if they would like to try something different or extra. Encourage them to ask for opportunities to demonstrate their worth.

(3) Thirdly, it is necessary to develop abilities and aptitudes to fill any gaps that are identified by (1) and (2). This is where straightforward on-the-job training and development helps, as long as it is planned and monitored correctly.

Well-motivated behaviour will usually result as long as people are well rewarded financially, given opportunities to express their abilities and allowed to grow so that they can realise their maximum potential. Management has a responsibility to see that all this happens. Let me repeat:

▶ *Motivated behaviour is a product of ability and opportunity:*

A word of warning: only give people opportunities if you want them to succeed. Unfortunately, I know managers who use opportunities as carrots, just to prove that some people are not capable of taking them.

This is the worst kind of management. Giving people opportunities and encouraging them during the learning processes associated with the opportunities is a straightforward way of developing them. It also increases their motivation on behalf of the organisation. It does, however take time and effort on the part of the manager. Remember:

 To develop people requires patience and understanding.

It is always better to withhold an opportunity if it is not possible to provide the support needed to help the individual make a success of it.

Consider the above points when you look at the performance sheet of a personnel manager; but first, a few words about the personnel/HR function.

HUMAN RESOURCES MANAGEMENT: A MISREPRESENTATION

Human relations in organisations have, over the last two decades, become more complex and formalised; some would claim too complex and formalised. The personnel/HR function, which once was mainly concerned with health and safety, now has to handle union negotiations, pension schemes, recruitment, redundancy, training, staff development, and wages and salaries grading. In most of the organisations I know, the personnel/HR function is regarded as a necessary evil. The personnel manager is, more often than not, the Cinderella of the management team—there just to act as a buffer between the managers with 'real' jobs to do and staff who won't always co-operate. Of course not all organisations, especially the big ones, use the personnel/HR function in such a way but for thousands of small organisations, that is the reality.

The personnel/HR manager does not usually manage many human resources at all. It is likely that such a manager will have very few staff and only limited authority. In most conventional production-based organisations it is the production manager that still really manages most of the human resources.

You can see from the above that in many organisations the personnel/HR department does not sit very comfortably with the other functional departments in many organisations. If you have a personnel/HR function, it must have teeth if it is to work positively. The personnel/HR manager must be a full and respected member of the management team and a full and contributing party to all the management team's decision processes. Personnel/HR managers must have an authority which fully matches the responsibilities the organisation places on them.

What is the situation in your organisation?

At first you may consider that the performance standard is too tight and over-fussy. Remember because of the special position of HR staff, it is essential that the personnel manager maintains a balance between the development of HR staff and the organisation's staff in general. For the HR/Personnel function to retain credibility, justice must be seen to be done.

By ensuring that training and development is co-ordinated with work-related activities, the performance standard also focuses on how the payback to the organisation is achieved.

JOB-SPECIFIC PROBLEMS: CAUSES AND SYMPTOMS

The next example covers *the 'core' management activity of the jackets off comrade.* You will remember that in Chapter One we suggested that all managers are required to

 Assist members of their team with job-specific problems.

In Chapter Two we also agreed that job-specific skills were required for the majority of managerial positions. In the context of 'jackets off comrade', this means:

(1) Experience and skills directly related to the work of team members, gained from actually doing the job.
(2) Previous training and development directly related to the specialist skills of team members.

Managers often think that they should be able to do the jobs of their team members better than any of the team. This is not the right way to approach assisting team members with problems. What a manager must have is a good understanding of the nature of the work of team members and how that work is interrelated. Let me be very clear on this point. There is a difference between assisting a team member with a problem and doing the job of the team member. Trying to take over the job of a team member in a problem situation may solve the immediate crisis but will not remove the long-term problem.

The example provided is taken from the performance sheet of a production manager. The example covers the day-to-day routine problems associated with setting up production runs in a multi-product organisation. However, before considering the production function and the

DEVELOPMENT GUIDE 13

'Core' Management Activity: Own Team Coach

EXAMPLE 4 THE PERSONNEL/HR MANAGER

JOB SEGMENT DESCRIPTION

(1) To prepare every year, with each member of the human resources team their personal training and development schedule (this schedule to be related to their current and proposed key tasks) by:
(a) One-to-one interviews. At each interview to consider and fully discuss prepared proposals from each team member regarding their personal training and development. To then agree a provisional timetable for the team member, covering both in-company and, if necessary, external training and development.

The proposals agreed at these interviews are to be co-ordinated with the proposals from all other departments to form the basis for the company's overall training and development plan.

(2) To present to, and agree with, the human resources team the department's training and development schedule for the coming 12 months including its integration with the company's overall training and development plan so as to:
(a) Ensure that the maximum support possible is available to other departments and there is a minimum disruption of duties [no more than one HR member of staff to be absent on personal training on any one day].
(b) Ensure that all training and development is co-ordinated with related work activities, thereby maximising the benefits both to the individual and to the organisation.

This is a difficult segment for the personnel/HR manager. It is a function of the personnel/HR department to provide training and development services for the rest of the organisation. In doing so HR staff may be deprived of opportunities for development themselves. The segment is designed to ensure that those who are responsible for training can also continue their own development. The segment provides the personnel/HR manager and HR team with an opportunity to balance the needs of everyone properly.

JOB SEGMENT PERFORMANCE STANDARD

Performance will be considered satisfactory if:

(1) Every 12 months one-to-one interviews are held with each member of the HR team to discuss and agree their personal training and development needs. These interviews must clarify how each HR team member's training is to be integrated into the organisation's overall training and development schedule.
(2) Every 12 months a provisional organisation development and training schedule is presented to the HR team for their endorsement and integration into the organisation's final development and training plan. This final plan must limit the release of HR team members for personal training to one per day.
(3) All agreed training and development activities are fully co-ordinated with work-related activities. The methods used for co-ordinating work and training activities must be agreed in writing by all the parties involved.

performance sheet of a production manager, we should first look at the nature of job specific problems in general.

We can all agree that managers have a responsibility to help their staff deal with job-specific problems; the range of such problems is of course endless. In my experience the main reasons for job-specific problems are as follows:

(1) Lack of organisational policies which advise staff how to act in specific circumstances relating to their work.
(2) Staff trying to achieve results using established but outdated organisational practices which management have failed to revise.
(3) Lack of on-the-job induction and development training, including management's failure to keep staff skills in line with the organisation's current technology.
(4) General lack of planned and appropriate training related to the introduction of new technology or methods of working.
(5) Ill-defined task instructions and definitions. These usually result from management's failure to carry out routine job analysis surveys to ensure that job descriptions are still relevant and appropriate.
(6) Tasks split across too many personnel. This is a very common fault in organisations that are contracting but still retain the job titles related to the old organisation structure.
(7) Poor routine supervisory guidance. This often results from supervisors being required to work as well as supervise.
(8) A genuine unexpected difficulty requiring experienced assistance.

From this list you can see that a pro-active manager can prevent seven out of every eight job specific problems ever arising by simply removing the cause of such problems. Remember:

▶ *Prevention rather than cure is the hallmark of the 'hands-on' manager.*

Unfortunately too many managers prefer to appear indispensable to their organisations by dealing with the symptoms rather than the causes of problems. They fail to instruct and train their staff properly and use any excuse to take over when the inevitable problems arise. Such practices result in continuing poor staff performance and an increase in the number of problems that are referred to management.

PROBLEM PREVENTION

You might find it useful to get your managers to consider the job-specific problems that have been referred to them over the last week. Get them to write them down in twenty minutes. If they need longer then they are probably taking over too often. Discuss with them how many of the problems could have been avoided by better policies, training, supervision, etc. You might also consider regularly reviewing job-specific problems as a team. Such a process will help keep your policies up to date and ensure that your training and supervision is being used to the organisation's best advantage.

DISCOVERY EXERCISE

Listing job-specific problems.   *Allow 20 minutes maximum.*

DISCUSSION EXERCISE

Discussing problem avoidance.   *Allow 60 minutes maximum.*

PRODUCTION: THE CORE OF THE BUSINESS

Without doubt the production function is the core of the business organisation apple. Remember that however good the organisation looks on the surface, if the core is bad so is the whole organisation.

Over the last twenty years developments in technology and industrial relations practices have changed the production function more than any other of the organisation's functions. These changes have created as many problems as they have solved. The leaders of organisations have often hurried to introduce new technologies in a reactive way, simply responding to fashion or foreign competition. This panic rather than planned approach has resulted in financial losses rather than gains, lost jobs and lost business opportunities. Let me give you an example of how not to manage new technology.

In 1981 I was asked to discover the reasons why a machine costing over £1.4 million was not being fully utilised more than two years after installation. The company involved produced stationery and was at the time one of the largest of its kind in the world. The machine involved was purchased to put lines on paper for note pads and stationery. To get the machine working the company had appointed a young fully trained and skilled 'liner'. They recruited this individual after a nationwide search. The young man had taken the job on the promise of a large increase in money and the prospects of a management position. At his previous employers he had produced very specialised ledgers, work which required a great degree of skill.

On the surface the young man's new job was straightforward and he had a small team of unskilled workers to help him. Unfortunately he soon found that the job was one of continuous job-specific problems. The production schedules were such that he had to keep up a constant supply of lined paper that bore no relation to the capabilities of the new machine. His immediate manager had over 450 workers to control and had no real interest in the problems of the new machine as long as the section could meet its production targets, 'After all he is the expert and should know what to do'. His unskilled workers could only achieve the required rate of production by using other small and very old machines. Nobody had a clear understanding of how to use the new machine and the previous supervisor had never shown the team members how to work it.

The young man was undaunted and set about finding out how the machine worked. The first thing he found was the instructions. Unfortunately these were all in German: no English version existed or had ever been requested. He then found out that the previous supervisor had been sent to Germany to learn how to operate the machine just six months before he was due to retire. When the young man complained about the lack of information on the new machine and requested help and changes in the methods of scheduling work he was branded as a trouble-maker.

It was only with great reluctance that the company agreed to my recommendation to send him to Germany for training, training which had to be paid for at full cost because only the original training had been included in the cost of the machine. While I was at this company I also found another machine covered over with sheets. This machine was a very advanced packaging machine that required a 2–inch gas main supply. The machine had never been made operational because, 'the required supply will not be available for at least two years'.

I realise that you may find the above example hard to believe. 'Surely', I hear you say, 'major public companies do not operate in such a way?' Well I am afraid some of them do and the problems described are all the result of bad management. The organisation concerned was over 70 years old and had been very profitable and successful. Unfortunately its very success had led it to believe it was above competition from smaller overseas operations and it had failed to plan the updating of its technology. Massive losses of market share had resulted in panic technology investments without the corresponding updating of management practices and work methods. The result was a complete disaster with job-specific problems in every functional area and major problems in production. At one stage the leaders even appointed two separate management consultancy firms to work within the company at the same time. As you can imagine this only made the situation worse.

WHAT SHOULD HAVE HAPPENED?

(1) Well, first, the time to plan new technology investments is when you are successful and your current technology is working well. This will allow you and your team to make a more objective assessment of what is available and to plan its introduction with the minimum of disruption.

(2) Next you must plan for the training that will be needed for the new technology and co-ordinate it with its installation. The sending of a supervisor for training on new technology just prior to his retirement must be regarded as gross managerial incompetence. Training must involve all the staff who will have to work in any way with the new technology. It is also important to monitor the results of all the training to ensure it is truly effective. Finally remember the best manufacturing machinery suppliers always provide comprehensive training. If none is offered then don't buy.

(3) There are always teething problems with new technology, so wherever possible new and old technology should be run side-by-side with a target date for the phasing out of the old. If you don't set a target date your people will probably find reasons for continuing with the old technology, so be strict about the length of this parallel running period.

(4) You must ensure that all activities related to the new technology, such as production scheduling, are checked for compatibility. This is essential managerial work.

(5) You should ensure that comprehensive documentation supporting the new technology is available for managerial interpretation at all times. Your managers should also set aside time for working with their team members during the initial stages of the new technology start-up. This will enable them to help sort out any job specific problems that arise.

(6) Finally, and very importantly, you must ensure that you are holding adequate finished stocks to cover for unforeseen problems with the new machinery. These stocks will allow your managers to take considered action in getting the new technology on stream rather than panic measures to meet customer demands.

THE KEY TO SUCCESSFUL PRODUCTION

To enjoy the same success as the Japanese in managing the production function requires investing in the best and most appropriate technology and investing in the best production workers. European workers are not really that much different from their Japanese counterparts but they are managed differently. Most new production technologies require fewer but more skilled 'thinking' workers. These 'thinking' workers require greater participation and need less supervision. Unfortunately many managers still find these facts hard to accept. They continue with the outmoded managerial practices that limit the contribution to the organisation's well-being that the new 'thinking' workers can make.

What is the situation in your organisation?

To make your production facility more effective don't over-man and don't over-supervise. Develop facilities for more shop-floor worker participation, employ better and fewer people and take a good look at quality circles. While you have been reading about the production facility at least 10 million Japanese workers have attended a quality circle meeting. Quality circles reduce the need for overt supervision, enhance the quality of products and improve the working life of shop-floor workers. The results of these meetings are there for everyone to see: look around your own home or office and you are almost certain to see the words 'Made in Japan'.

The final managerial key segment example covers

THE 'CORE' MANAGEMENT ACTIVITY: WAVING THE FLAG CHEER-LEADER.

You will remember that in Chapter One we agreed that all managers are required to

REPRESENT THEIR AREA OF RESPONSIBILITY ON BEHALF OF THE ORGANISATION.

Some managers consider this activity to be the prime function of management and spend a high percentage of their time representing rather than really managing. My research indicates that today's most effective managers try to confine this activity to around 15% of their total time.

The example I provide is taken from the performance sheet of a general manager, that is, a manager who is senior to the key functional managers in an organisation. The example concerns the meetings that seem to form a major part of life in most organisations. In addition to the meetings which most managers seem destined to have to attend, there are a number of other activities which can be loosely grouped under this heading. They are:

(1) Giving after-dinner and luncheon speeches at business-related functions.
(2) Saying 'Thank you and goodbye' to long-serving members of staff.
(3) Sitting on the committees of professional bodies, employer's organisations and educational institutions.
(4) Representing the organisation at public meetings and enquiries.

DEVELOPMENT GUIDE 14

'Core' Management Activity: Jackets off comrade

EXAMPLE 5 THE PRODUCTION MANAGER

JOB SEGMENT DESCRIPTION

To walk the production floor at least three times every working week of the year. Each time to spend at least 90 minutes on the production floor being seen by and accessible to production floor management [supervisors and foremen] and workers, to listen to and assist with job-specific and, when necessary, personal problems.

PERFORMANCE STANDARDS

Performance will be considered satisfactory if:

(1) Investigation of any job-specific problem reveals that it received managerial attention within 12 hours of occurring.

(2) Time is set aside at each production manager-led production floor meeting to investigate and remove the causes of any management-notified job-specific problems that may have arisen since the last meeting.

(3) All job-specific problems are dealt with by the immediate senior of the individual raising the problem.

This key job segment is both simple and straightforward. The production manager must not hide behind an office door or glass partition. Successful production management requires having a current, first-hand understanding of what is going on in the constantly changing production environment. The problems of the shop-floor workers must not be allowed to fester and grow out of proportion. If this recommended approach is adopted management, not the union representatives, will be in control of the production shop floor. There is a place for the union representative but it is not running the show.

I am sure you can think of further examples. In general the 'figurehead role' of the manager, as Henry Mintzberg describes it in his book *The Nature of Managerial Work*, has grown in dimension and can, if care is not taken to restrict it, dominate a manager's life. In many ways the activity has a PR dimension, concerned as it is with maintaining the good name or standing of the area under the manager's control. It is important to remember that people often arrive at their perception of an organisation or department from how a manager represents it.

MEETINGS, BLOODY MEETINGS

I hope you have seen the two Video Arts films on meetings. *Meetings Bloody Meetings* and its follow-up *More Bloody Meetings* say more about the reality of modern managerial life than a thousand managerial textbooks. I strongly recommend that you take the first opportunity to view them again and then consider the situation in your own organisation. Remember:

ALL MEETINGS ABSORB MONEY, TIME AND ENERGY. ONLY 50% OF MEETINGS ARE REALLY NECESSARY AND ONLY 25% OF MEETINGS HAVE A POSITIVE PAYBACK.

In autocratic, closed organisations meetings are necessary for even the most minor of actions and managers must attend to defend their areas of interest. In organisations which encourage participation and openness 'waving the flag cheer-leader' activities tend to be less in demand and are shared.

What type of organisation is yours?

If an analysis of the activity diaries of your managers shows that they are spending more than 20% of their time in meetings then you have a problem. Even if your managers are spending less than 20% of their time at meetings the time they are spending may be largely wasted. The way to assess this is straightforward as the following exercise shows.

DISCOVERY EXERCISE

Appraisal of the effectiveness of meetings.   *Allow 30 minutes.*

DEVELOPMENT GUIDE 15

Meetings, Bloody Meetings: Effectiveness Appraisal

Name: [Department/section:]

This exercise concerns meetings and how effective they are in furthering the work of your area of responsibility. If you have just completed an activity diary use the data from the diary for the exercise. If you do not have activity diary data then use your best judgement and get your secretary or assistant to check your responses. Try to answer as accurately as you possibly can.

QUESTIONS

(1) How many meetings did you attend during the last full working month?

(2) How much time on average did you spend at each of these meetings?

(3) What % of the total average time you spent at meetings did you spend making an active contribution?

(4) How many of the meetings had more than 12 participants?

(5) How many of the meetings lasted more than 90 minutes?

(6) Write down on separate sheets of paper the three main items you think were achieved at each meeting. Be as brief as you can.

(7) What was the total of items achieved at the meetings you attended during the month?

(8) Write down next to each main item what you think was achieved, whether or not it concerned directly the work of your area.

(9) What was the total of items achieved that directly concerned the work of your area?

DEVELOPMENT GUIDE 15

Meetings, Bloody Meetings: Effectiveness Appraisal

Consider the information on this page in conjunction with your answers to the questions on the previous page. The information is designed to help you to improve your effectiveness in using management time in relation to meetings.

QUESTION (1)   If you attended more than 12 meetings you need to assess very carefully whether you really needed to attend all of the meetings you did. Consider these points:
(a) Were there items on each meeting's agenda that concerned you and your department?
(b) Could you have delegated attendance at some of the meetings to members of your team?
(c) Could you have dealt with the items that concerned your area by phone or one-to-one interview?

QUESTIONS (2) and (3)   If the average time you spent at each meeting was more than 60 minutes and the time you were actively contributing was less than 30 minutes then you probably wasted 25% of your time. Consider these points:
(a) Could you have left after your contribution?
(b) Could your contribution have been made in writing rather than by attendance?

QUESTION (4)   If more than 12 people attend meetings they are assemblies rather than meetings and everyone is probably wasting a lot of their time. The most effective size for a meeting is up to eight people.

QUESTION (5)   If the majority of meetings you attended lasted more than 90 minutes then at least 20% of the items could have been dealt with better by telephone or one-to-one discussions. You should seek to limit meetings to 90 minutes at all times.

QUESTION (6)   The meetings which did not decide three items were likely to have been unnecessary and you shouldn't have been at the meetings you can't remember.

QUESTIONS (7), (8) and (9)   If less than 60% of the items concerned your department you need not have attended 40% of the meetings.

Finally, remember that if a meeting is called without an agenda try and avoid attending. If the items on the agenda interest you rather than concern your area just obtain a copy of the minutes, do not attend.

THE GENERAL MANAGER: FULCRUM OF THE MANAGEMENT TEAM

Make no mistake about it, the role of general manager is the most difficult in management. The job requires judgement, tact, foresight, firmness and great inter-personal skills, all at the same time. Many top functional managers just never make it as general managers: they can't make the transition from specialist to generalist. Balancing the priorities of the organisation against the wishes and well-argued plans of functional specialists is the continuing task of the general manager. This task has to be achieved while retaining the support of those whose ideas and plans are not always seen as organisationally the most appropriate. Successful general managers seem to have a flair for this balancing act and manage to repeat it time and again.

Organisations who appoint their best specialist or functional managers as general managers are often disappointed. The best general managers are rarely the best at their specialisation although they are always very competent. If they were finance specialists they tended to reveal rather than maintain the mystique of figures. If they were production specialists they were usually able to understand the marketing department's viewpoint. It is this wider perceptual ability that separates the general manager from the functional whizz-kid. Always being able to take an organisation-wide viewpoint is the main criterion for successful general management.

In the successful organisation we are creating, the role of general manager is the most important. It is the general manager who provides the impetus and example to all the other managers. He or she will be the most 'hands on' manager in the organisation. In addition to the main skills of management this manager will have the following key qualities:

(1) A clear understanding and knowledge of how all the functional areas of the organisation work and interrelate.

(2) A clear understanding and knowledge of the total environment in which the organisation has to operate.

(3) The ability and skill to harness the combined energies of the management team so as to maximise the resulting synergy on behalf of the organisation.

(4) The ability and skill to maintain and utilise the external relationships needed by the organisation for continued success.

(5) The ability and skill to retain the support of all the stakeholders of the organisation through difficult operating times.

(6) And finally, a really good general manager will, from day one, be actively developing a successor.

DEVELOPMENT GUIDE 16

'Core' Management Activity: Waving The Flag Cheer Leader

EXAMPLE 6 THE GENERAL MANAGER

JOB SEGMENT DESCRIPTION

(1) To assess each month, with members of the management team, the senior management meetings schedule, both internal and external, for the coming month; to agree with each manager who should attend which meetings, what can be delegated; and to ensure that no manager, including the general manager, attends more than 12 meetings over the month.

It is a requirement of this job segment that the reasons for each and every meeting are fully explored and every effort is made to ensure that no unnecessary meetings take place.

(2) To assess each month the 'figurehead' tasks required of senior management and allocate these across the senior management team so as to ensure that no manager spends more than 10% of time on these activities.

JOB SEGMENT PERFORMANCE STANDARD

(1) Performance will be considered satisfactory if the number of meetings attended by the senior management team does not exceed an average of more than 12 meetings per manager, including the general manager, per month.

(2) Performance will be considered satisfactory if the hours spent by senior managers on 'figurehead' activities do not average more than 4 hours per week for any single manager, including the general manager.

The results of this job segment can be more far-reaching than at first they appear to be. The segment forces delegation from the general manager right down through senior management to the teams of each functional and specialist manager. It reduces the 'charismatic' leader effect and consequences and increases the opportunities people have to make decisions and contribute to meetings. It also ensures that all meetings have a purpose.

CHAPTER SUMMARY

We have now reached the half-way stage in the development of the 'hands on' manager. Each chapter so far has been designed as a building-block in the individual management development process.

By working your way through Chapter One, you and your managers should have come to terms with the actuality of the work of managers in your organisation. As a result, changes in approach, style and the way managerial time is used in your organisation should all have started to occur.

By working your way through Chapter Two, you and your managers should have come to terms with the individual strengths and weaknesses that exist in your management team. As a result your managers should have started to reduce the negative effects of their identified weaknesses. You should have also started to evolve plans and strategies for developing and enhancing the managerial aptitudes of your management team members.

You and your managers should now make a concerted effort to adapt the key job segment examples found in this chapter so that they suit the specific task and performance needs of your organisation. A pro-forma 'hands on' performance sheet is provided at the end of this chapter for your guidance. Your objective should be to ensure that:

(1) Every manager in your organisation knows exactly what are the key segments of their management job.

(2) Every manager in your organisation knows what they have to do to perform the tasks making up those key segments to the required standard.

(3) Every manager in your organisation knows how long they have to reach the required and agreed standards and when those standards will be reviewed jointly with you.

When you have achieved this objective you will have completed all the foundation work necessary to introduce successful 'hands on' management into your organisation. Your next task will then be to evolve and enhance the system so that it continues to meet the specific needs of your organisation. Remember that for the system to work it must remain dynamic. The following chapters are designed to help you maintain and further enhance the effectiveness of your management.

COMPLETING THE KEY JOB SEGMENTS

Figure 7 is a blank 'hands on' job segment description and performance sheet. Use this in conjunction with the completed development guides from this chapter to write up the key segments of your management job. Remember your job should mainly contain activities that relate to the five core managerial activities described in both Chapter One and this chapter.

When writing up your performance sheets try to keep things brief, specific and measurable. To help you achieve this the following guidelines are provided.

(1) When writing up a job segment always start with the word '*to*'. For example:
(a) To meet with staff once a month.
(b) To discuss problems of a job-specific nature.

(2) Avoid general words when you are writing down something which has to be measured, for example:
(a) 'To meet *regularly*' would be better expressed as: 'To meet on [insert date]'.
(b) 'To maintain *good* standards of work' would be better expressed as: 'To maintain standards of work to the *agreed* [or following] specification'.

(3) The performance standard(s) must be written so that they contain the method and timing of the performance measurement; for example:
(a) Performance will be considered satisfactory if a *report* covering progress is submitted every *three weeks*.
(b) Performance will be considered satisfactory if a *meeting* is held every *month* to agree targets.

Note: Writing up job segments is time-consuming and requires careful consideration. Only carry out this work when you can give it the time and attention it deserves. Like all worthwhile things in life it is not easy or straightforward but long term it is very beneficial. Good luck!

NAME . . . .

ORGANISATION . . . .

JOB TITLE . . . .

JOB SEGMENT No . . . . DESCRIPTION . . . .
. . . .

To . . . .

. . . .

. . . .

. . . .

. . . .

. . . .

. . . .

. . . .

. . . .

. . . .

JOB SEGMENT No . . . . PERFORMANCE STANDARD
Performance will be considered satisfactory if: . . . .

. . . .

. . . .

. . . .

. . . .

. . . .

. . . .

. . . .

. . . .

THIS JOB SEGMENT AND PERFORMANCE STANDARD WILL BE REVIEWED ON
(DATE) . . . .

FIG. 7. JOB SEGMENT DESCRIPTION AND PERFORMANCE.

4

BUILDING THE MANAGEMENT TEAM

A management team is not likely to succeed unless it can utilise all the individual talents of its members to the maximum advantage of the organisation.

This chapter is designed to help you create a winning management team. The eight key management team roles are introduced, along with the individual characteristics and attributes necessary to perform these roles. Finally consideration is given to the integration of the various roles and the creation of the right 'team mix'.

Reference will be made to the personal characteristics and strengths of each of your managers, originally discussed in Chapter Two. This time your managers will be asked to consider their strengths and weaknesses in relation to the defined management team roles. This process should enable you and your managers to look at ways of improving the team's cohesion and building it into the most effective and efficient component of your organisation.

By the end of the chapter each of your managers should be able to identify clearly the role to which they are best suited in your management team. This in turn will enable you to use each manager in team situations to the maximum advantage of the organisation. The process of identifying management team roles will reveal present or future gaps in the team's overall composition. When you are ready to recruit new members, you will have the information you need to select those who will complement and enhance your team. By building your team in this way you will have achieved another significant objective in the development of the 'hands on' manager; that is:

The development of managers who are as efficient and effective management team members as they are individual managers.

THE TEAM AND SUCCESS

By now you will appreciate that the complexities of your modern organisation and the world it operates in require more than just one or two dynamic personalities to enable it to be successful. All organisations that want to win need managers who can work together, not just as talented individuals but as a team; that is, a team capable of generating the positive synergy that always seems to be present in the really successful organisations, especially when the going gets tough.

Unfortunately, winning teams cannot be created easily. It is not just a question of hiring talent: many chequebook-waving football managers have discovered this the hard way. Winning teams have to be built up and developed with both care and foresight over a period of time. You need to have a clear picture of what you want the team to be able to do. Each member of the team has to know what their role is and how it fits in with the roles of the other team members. The team then has to work together to arrive at the best pattern of operation. All these things take time and even when you have developed things the way you want them, there will be a further delay before you experience the full benefits. A football analogy will illustrate the point. The winning edge Liverpool football team produces against competing teams is not good fortune. Liverpool's success is the result of long-term manpower planning and development, balanced teamwork and an evolved commitment to the team above everything else. For Liverpool football players it is being part of the team that really counts. Remember:

SUCCESSFUL TEAMS ARE COMMITTED TEAMS.

THE INDIVIDUAL MANAGER AND THE MANAGEMENT TEAM

The first two problems to deal with in creating a winning team are individuality and individual interests. Both are very much products of our western world and culture. Rather than trying to overcome these problems, turn them to your advantage in building the team.

You have gone out of your way to recruit and develop talented individuals for specific roles in your organisation. They have special areas of responsibility that you want them to champion. These are features you don't want to lose. You now want them to work together, appreciate each other's problems and the needs of each other's areas of interest. This is an extra dimension to their job and should be treated as such. The only way they are willingly going to take on this extra dimension is if it is in their best interests to do so. Your job is to convince them that they will achieve more for themselves and their areas of responsibility by working together than they will on their own. They have to be convinced of the benefits of positive synergy.

TOWARDS A TEAM APPROACH: 'wa'

Unfortunately for western industry, when it comes to working effectively in management teams the Japanese have a head start. Individuality and self-interest are not strong features of oriental culture and from day one they have a deep appreciation of interdependence. The Japanese call this form of interdependence 'wa'. The literal translation of 'wa' is 'group harmony' but it also means 'unity', 'team spirit' and the sort of cohesion that makes the modern Japanese organisation such a formidable competitor.

HOW MUCH 'wa' DOES YOUR ORGANISATION HAVE?

I would now like you to consider the degree of 'wa' that exists in your organisation by doing a simple exercise. In the last chapter we considered meetings and I suggested ways of controlling the number of meetings needed in your organisation. 'Wa' is most likely to be overtly displayed in your organisation at meetings, so I want you to think back over your last few management meetings; that is, meetings devoted solely to the management of your organisation and its strategic outlook.

(1) Think about the decisions that were reached and the way they were reached. Are you really satisfied that everyone left the meeting 100% committed to the strategic decisions reached?

(2) Think about the commitment to and support for the decisions given by each member of your team. Are you really satisfied with the quality of support given?

(3) Think about the appreciation of the problems of their colleagues that was shown by various managers. Are you really satisfied that everyone showed a concern for and behaved in the best long-term interests of the organisation as a whole?

Now write down your feelings about those meetings and in the light of what I have said about team work and 'wa', decide how much 'wa' exists in your organisation and between your managers. Is there room for improvement?

DISCOVERY EXERCISE

Deciding the degree of 'wa' in your organisation.   *Allow 25 minutes.*

MEETINGS: THE WESTERN MANAGERIAL BATTLEGROUND

I would like to continue this examination of the quality of your management meetings, particularly those concerned with your organisation's strategic outlook. In an organisation that is managed by team-work these meetings form the major means of communication between managers. In Japan and Hong Kong, for example, meetings are long, drawn-out affairs. Battles are rare and the showing of mutual respect is a significant part of the ritual of meetings there. Japanese managers use meetings to make key decisions and to establish 100% commitment to those decisions. Nobody leaves the room until everybody is 100% committed; if that is not possible, no decision is made. These points are significant factors in the quality of oriental decision-making. Every aspect of the subject requiring a decision is explored. Everyone has to be involved and every one has to be committed. The decisions are a long time coming but they nearly always work.

In the last twenty-five years I have been to many hundreds of western management meetings and most of them have contained elements of one or more of the following:

(1) At least one heated argument which could only be resolved by the chairman's intervention.

(2) The resigned or grudging acceptance of majority views or decisions by an obviously disappointed minority.

(3) The planned trading-off of support between some managers against the views of others to win points and get their own way.

(4) The reaching of compromise decisions which in reality satisfied nobody.

(5) The surprise introduction of information or important data in attempts to belittle other managers; often this is information everyone should have had an opportunity to consider well before the meeting.

(6) The sabotaging of an individual's pet project or idea in revenge for similar but reversed situations at earlier meetings.

(7) A lack of real commitment to 75% of what is taking place by those attending because it concerns areas that they do not see as directly affecting them.

From this, you can see why I was so keen in the last chapter to reduce the time spent on meetings in your organisation. The western cult of the individual tends to breed situations similar to those I have described and must be controlled.

The traditional western answer to the battleground behaviour described, is even worse. The leaders of some organisations have meetings which are not really meetings at all: they are assemblies to hear the words of the 'prophet'. At these 'prophet' meetings the chairman and those few managers who help maintain the chairman's power do all the talking. They tell the other managers what is going to happen, who is going to do what and then dare the assembled managers to comment. Any manager who is foolish enough to question the decisions is likely to be asked to stay behind and explain their behaviour.

As neither of these western approaches are what you need for the winning organisation you are building, we will now start work on the western version of 'wa' and develop management teams capable of meeting together constructively.

THE KEY MANAGEMENT TEAM ROLES

Let's start the process of building a positive management team by considering the range of management team roles that are possible. There is no ideal management team size; it depends largely on your organisation and its structure. What can be said is that you start to lose effectiveness when you reach double figures. In reality you move into the 'assembly' syndrome.

The Japanese can work effectively in larger numbers but at this point in time I doubt whether western managers can. Western teams of three, five, seven and eight can all be developed to work well.

THE 16PF AND DR BELBIN

In Chapter Two we saw how using the 16PF can provide information about the characteristics and qualities of our managers. Data from the 16PF can also be used to identify your manager's preferred management team roles.

In 1981 a book by Dr Meredith Belbin, *Management Teams: Why they Succeed or Fail*, was published. Dr Belbin used data from the 16PF to identify eight key preferred management team roles. Other key roles in management teams have been identified. In Australia, for example, Prof. Charles Margerison has developed a set of roles under nine headings. He also defines five key functions that management teams and their leaders perform: *advising, organising, controlling, exploring and linking* [the leader's role]. When you read the key management-team role definitions on the next few pages you will see how easily the roles can be placed under those headings.

THE DUAL ROLE PROBLEM

There is one major point that must be made about the roles managers like to play in teams. Remember:

REGARDLESS OF THEIR PREFERRED ROLE IN THE ORGANISATON'S MANAGEMENT TEAM, ALL MANAGERS MUST ALSO REPRESENT THEIR AREA OF AUTHORITY.

This means they have to be both team leaders and members of the main management team. This duel role is often overlooked but it is crucial. For example, suppose a manager likes to play an active and aggressive role in the management team. That manager's approach is likely to be similar when he or she is representing his or her own particular area of authority. But while an aggressive stance may be appropriate when the team is planning the strategic future of the organisation, it may be less so when functional budgets and resources allocation matters are being discussed.

Only when the senior executive generates and maintains a high level of commitment to the organisation's overall well-being can this problem be tackled. Each member of the management team must learn to appreciate the need for all areas of responsibility to be treated equally so that they can function only in the best interests of the organisation as a whole. This requires a considerable degree of managerial maturity, something often lacking in otherwise very successful managers.

THE FUNCTIONAL MANAGER'S DILEMMA

It takes a really mature manager to go back to the team and advise them they will not be receiving the resources they counted on. Especially when the reason is, as a member of the organisation's management team, you decided the money for the resources would be better spent elsewhere.

THE EIGHT BELBIN-PREFERRED MANAGEMENT TEAM ROLES

On the next few pages you will find my interpretations of the eight Belbin preferred management team roles. You and your managers should read each description carefully to gain a full understanding of the qualities of each role.

After you have read the role descriptions you will find further information on how to use the information to build your management team is provided.

DEVELOPMENT GUIDE 17

Dr Belbin's key management Team Roles*

THE CHAIRMAN

ROLE

The Chairman likes the role of controlling the way in which the management team works to achieve the organisation's objectives. The Chairman carries out this role by tapping into all of the management team's resources. A good Chairman will be able to recognise where the management team's strengths and weaknesses lie and will ensure that the best use is made of each team member's potential.

ATTRIBUTES

Strengths:
(a) An ability to command respect and to inspire enthusiasm.
(b) A first-class sense of timing and balance, coupled with a capacity for communicating easily with others.

Tolerable weaknesses:
No very marked creative or intellectual power.

Traits:
Stable, dominant, and slightly extrovert.

GENERAL DETAIL

Chairman, or more properly Chairperson, is a slightly misleading title, as the Chairman may well not be the leader of the management team. Leadership is, however, what Chairmen are best fitted for. Chairmen have, at the very least, a normal level of intelligence but would not fall into the brilliant category; neither are they usually outstanding creative thinkers. It is rare for good, creative ideas to originate from Chairmen.

Chairmen are more remarkable for what is called 'character'; their approach is disciplined, and this is founded on self-discipline. They often have 'charisma' and an air of authority. They are dominant, but in a relaxed and unassertive way; they are not usually domineering.

The Chairman's first instinct is to trust people unless there is very strong evidence that they are untrustworthy. They rarely display jealousy.

Chairmen are able to talk easily and are usually easy to talk to. They are good two-way communicators, being neither compulsive talkers nor people of few words. They are certainly very good listeners.

DEVELOPMENT GUIDE 18

Dr Belbin's key management Team Roles

THE SHAPER

ROLE

The Shaper likes to shape the way in which the team's effort is applied. The Shaper will direct attention generally to the setting of organisational objectives and priorities. The Shaper will also seek to impose some pattern on the management team's discussions and the outcome of the management team's activities.

ATTRIBUTES

Strengths:
Drive and self-confidence.

Tolerable weaknesses:
Intolerance towards vague ideas and people.

Traits:
Anxious, dominant, extrovert.

GENERAL DETAIL

Some observers of management teams in action have suggested that a successful management team needs a 'social' leader, who is the permanent head of the team and a separate 'task' leader, who is in charge of a specific and defined project. If this is true then Shapers are the 'task' leaders and Chairmen are the 'social' leaders. Shapers are most likely to be actual leaders of management teams in cases where there is no Chairman, or where the Chairman is not in fact the leader.

Shapers are full of nervous energy, outgoing and emotional, impulsive and impatient. They are easily frustrated. They are quick to challenge and quick to respond to a challenge. In general they enjoy and welcome challenges. They often have rows, but they are quickly over and Shapers do not generally harbour grudges.

Of all the members of the management team the Shaper is the most prone to paranoia, quick to sense a slight and the first to feel that there is a conspiracy afoot of which they are the object or victim.

The principle function of the Shaper is to give a shape to the application of the management team's efforts, often supplying more personal input than the Chairman. They are always looking for a pattern in discussions and trying to unite ideas, objectives and practical considerations into a single feasible project. They will then urgently seek to push the project forward for final decision and action.

Shapers often display great self-confidence which may hide strong self-doubt. Only results can reassure the Shaper. The Shaper's drive, which has a compulsive quality, is always directed at the attainment of personal objectives. These objectives are usually also the management team's objectives, but then Shapers often see their management teams as extensions of themselves and their own egos.

Shapers usually want action and they 'want it now'. They are personally competitive, intolerant of vagueness and muddled thinking. People outside the management team are likely to describe Shapers as arrogant and abrasive. Even people inside the team are in danger of being steamrollered by the Shaper on occasions, and they can make the team uncomfortable.

The Shaper's key attribute is making things happen.

DEVELOPMENT GUIDE 19

Dr Belbin's key management Team Roles*

THE COMPANY WORKER

ROLE

The Company Worker likes to turn concepts and plans into practical working procedures. The Company Worker will lead the effort in seeing to it that the management team's agreed plans are carried out systematically and efficiently.

ATTRIBUTES

Strengths:
Self-control and self-discipline combined with realism and practical commonsense.

Tolerable weaknesses:
Lack of flexibility and an unresponsiveness to new ideas that remain unproven.

Traits:
Stable and controlled

GENERAL DETAIL

Company Workers are the practical organisers on the management team. They translate all the concepts and ideas into practical, down-to-earth tasks and get on with them logically and loyally.

Company Workers, have, like Chairmen, a strength of character and a disciplined approach. They are notable for sincerity, integrity, and trust of colleagues, and are not easily deflated or discouraged. It is only a sudden change of plan that is likely to upset them, because they are liable to flounder in unstable, quickly changing situations.

Because Company Workers need stable structures, they are always trying to build them. Give them a decision and they will produce a schedule, give them a group of people and an objective and they will produce an organisation chart.

Company Workers work efficiently, systematically, and methodically, but sometimes a little inflexibly, and they are often unresponsive to speculative airy-fairy ideas that do not have visible immediate bearing on the task in hand.

DEVELOPMENT GUIDE 20

Dr Belbin's key management Team Roles*

THE MONITOR-EVALUATOR

ROLE

The role the Monitor Evaluator likes to play in a management team is the one that involves analysing problems and evaluating ideas and suggestions. Success in this role ensures that the management team is better placed to take balanced decisions.

ATTRIBUTES

Strengths:
Effective thinking ability of a high order, including the ability to see the complications of proposals. The Monitor Evaluator has a very objective mind.

Tolerable weaknesses:
Hypercritical, unexciting and a little over-serious.

Traits:
High IQ, introvert, stable.

GENERAL DETAIL

Monitor Evaluators are usually capable of carrying out deep and dispassionate analyses of huge quantities of data. They are slow, stable, introvert and tend to lack imagination and vision.

Monitor Evaluators are unlikely to come up with original proposals but they are the management team members who are most likely to stop the team from committing itself to a misguided project. Sometimes, they can do this in a tactless and disparaging way. This does not raise their popularity amongst team members. Their approach can also, on occasions, lower the team's morale if they apply too much discouragement at the wrong time.

Although Monitor Evaluators are solid and dependable, they lack warmth, imagination and spontaneity. Nevertheless, they have one quality which makes them indispensable to the management team—their judgement is hardly ever wrong.

DEVELOPMENT GUIDE 21

Dr Belbin's key management Team Roles*

THE TEAM WORKER

ROLE

The role the Team Worker likes most is supporting the other management team members. The Team Worker likes to help develop the different team members' strengths by building on their suggestions. They will also underpin any shortcomings in other team members by improving communications between members and fostering team spirit generally.

ATTRIBUTES

Strengths:
Humility, flexibility, popularity and good listening skills.

Tolerable weaknesses:
Lack of decisiveness and toughness; a distaste for friction and competition.

Traits:
Stable, extrovert, submissive.

GENERAL DETAIL

Team Workers are usually the most sensitive members of the management team. They are the ones who are most aware of the individual needs and worries of team members, and are likely to perceive most clearly the emotional undercurrent within the management team.

Team Workers usually know the most about the private lives and family affairs of the rest of the management team.

Team Workers are good and willing listeners and communicate freely and well within the team. They also help and encourage others to do the same.

As the promoters of unity and harmony, Team Workers counterbalance the friction and discord that can be caused by Shapers and Plants. They are exemplary team members and though in normal times the value of their contribution may not be as immediately visible as that of most of the other management team roles, the effect is very noticeable when they are not there, especially in times of stress and pressure.

DEVELOPMENT GUIDE 22

Dr Belbin's key management Team Roles*

THE RESOURCE INVESTIGATOR

ROLE

The Resource Investigator likes the role of exploring and reporting on ideas, developments and resources outside the immediate area of the management team. The Resource Investigator will create the external contacts that may be useful to the team, and will usually conduct any of the subsequent negotiations.

ATTRIBUTES

Strengths:
Will have an outgoing, relaxed personality with a strong inquisitive sense, and a readiness to see the possibilities inherent in anything new.

Tolerable weaknesses:
Will be inclined towards over-enthusiasm and a lack of follow-up.

Traits:
Stable, dominant, extrovert.

GENERAL DETAIL

Resource Investigators are usually very amiable characters. They either have six phones on the go or are out making contacts. They are the management team's PR, big ears, and diplomats in the outside world.

Resource Investigators are likely to be relaxed, sociable, and gregarious, with interests that are easily aroused. Their responses tend to be positive and enthusiastic, though they are prone to put things down as quickly as they take them up.

Without the stimulus of others, for example in a solitary job, Resource Investigators can easily become bored, demoralised and ineffective.

DEVELOPMENT GUIDE 23

Dr Belbin's key management Team Roles*

THE COMPLETER-FINISHER

ROLE

The Completer Finisher likes the role of ensuring that the management team is protected as far as possible from errors of commission and omission. The Completer Finisher searches for aspects of the management team's work which may need a more than usual degree of attention. They also will maintain that sense of urgency within the management team which is needed to achieve results.

ATTRIBUTES

Strengths:
Will have an ability to combine a sense of concern with a sense of order and purpose; self-control and strength of character.

Tolerable weaknesses:
Will be inclined to be impatient and intolerant towards those of casual disposition and habits.

Traits:
Anxious, introvert.

GENERAL DETAIL

Completer Finishers are sticklers for detail, deadlines and schedules; they are always worrying about what might go wrong.

Completer Finishers are never happy or at ease until they have personally checked every detail and made sure that everything has been done and nothing overlooked. It must be said that it is not that Completer Finishers are overtly or irritatingly fussy, their obsession is an expression of anxiety.

The Completer Finisher's main preoccupation is that of order. They are compulsive meeters of deadlines and fulfillers of schedules.

On the management team the Completer Finisher can be rather depressing, but as the management team's professional 'worrier', the Completer Finisher's relentless follow-through is crucial.

DEVELOPMENT GUIDE 24

Dr Belbin's key management Team Roles*

THE PLANT

ROLE

The Plant likes to advance new ideas and strategies. The Plant will pay special attention to major issues and look for different approaches to the problems with which the management team is confronted.

ATTRIBUTES

Strengths:
Independence of outlook, high intelligence and imagination.

Traits:
Dominant, very high IQ, introvert.

Tolerable weaknesses:
A tendency to be impractical or to be 'up in the clouds' at times and sometimes to be weak in communicating with others.

GENERAL DETAIL

Plants are the team's source of original ideas, suggestions and proposals; they are ideas people. Of course other team members have ideas; what distinguishes the Plant's ideas is their originality and the lateral approach they bring to problems and obstacles.

Plants are the most imaginative as well as the most intelligent members of the management team. Plants are the most likely team members to start searching for a completely new approach to a problem especially if the team gets bogged down. They will often bring a new insight to a line of action already agreed.

Plants are more concerned with major issues and fundamentals than with details and indeed they are likely to miss out on details and make careless mistakes. They are trustful and uninhibited in a way that is fairly uncharacteristic of an introvert and are sometimes regarded as extrovert.

Plants can be prickly and cause offence to other members of the team particularly when criticising their ideas. Their criticisms are often designed to clear the ground for their own ideas and are usually followed by their counter-proposals.

The danger with Plants is that they will devote too much of their creative energy to ideas which may catch their fancy but do not fall in with the team's needs or contribute to its objectives. They may be bad at accepting criticism of their own ideas and quick to take offence and sulk if their ideas are dissected or rejected. They may even switch off and refuse to make any further contribution.

It can take quite a lot of careful handling and judicious flattery to get the best out of a Plant. But for all their faults, it is the Plants who provide the vital spark.

USING THE PREFERRED TEAM ROLES TO BUILD THE TEAM

If both you and your management team have completed the 16PF and have received second-order factors results which consider the Belbin team roles, you will find the next stage is straightforward. (NB. A separate computer program from the PCDP is needed to generate the Belbin second-order factor scores.)

The first task is to get each manager to read the detail of the role or roles for which their second-order factor scores are high and assess the relevance of the same. For example, compare my second-order Belbin scores with those that would be generated from the 'ideal manager's' 16PF:

	Bill Watts	'Ideal Manager'
Chairman	7.5	9.7
Shaper	5.4	5.8
Company Worker	3.6	7.0
Monitor Evaluator	2.6	5.5
Team Worker	4.9	5.4
Resource Investigator	9.1	8.8
Completer	4.1	6.6
Plant	9.7	8.5

You can see from these scores that three roles are really preferred by me: number one—Plant; number two—Resource Investigator; and number three—Chairman. All the rest do not count. This surprises some people who like to regard me as a Shaper. The combination of the characteristics of a Resource Investigator and Plant is an odd but quite formidable one and gives rise to Shaper-like behaviour on occasions, especially when I can't get my own way.

The 'ideal manager's' 16PF second-order factors scores reveal four preferred roles: number one—Chairman; number two—Resource Investigator; number three—Plant; and number four—Company Worker. The 'ideal manager' therefore has a well-balanced group of preferences indicating good leadership qualities plus the ability to look outside the group and get the task done.

Once you and your managers have read and re-read the suggested preferred team roles' descriptions, discuss the accuracy of the roles' descriptions generated from the 16PF data as a group. If the highest scores are only 6+ then the role preference is not likely to be too great and in fact the desire for team membership in general is probably weak.

If you are satisfied that the descriptions are a reasonable fit you can then look for gaps or overlaps in the team's composition and then judge how crucial they are. For example, if you have three Shapers with scores of 9+ in a team of seven you have a real problem and I doubt whether your management team can ever be made to work properly over any long period of time. Equally, if your team does not have a Plant then it may lack the extra intellectual input it needs to place it in a winning position. Whatever your immediate reactions, spend some time and thought comparing your team's composition with its suggested composition. Ask yourself how team members actually perform before making any changes.

NON-16PF RESULT COMPARISONS

If you and your team haven't completed the 16PF then you are faced with a more subjective management-team role appraisal. Get each member of your team to select the description which they consider most closely describes their management team role, scoring each 1 to 10. Once they have finished get them to score each other. If you keep the whole thing secret, until everybody has scored themselves and everybody else, you will have a good basis for a very interesting team discussion. You will also be able to assess, with some degree of accuracy, the gaps and overlaps that exist in your management team.

WINNING TEAMS, WORKING TEAMS

What mix of Belbin-preferred team roles makes a winning team? There is no clear answer to that question since different situations and organisations need different mixes. However, over a period of five years, both in simulation situations and in actual organisations, I have experimented with different mixes and have found that there are certain combinations you must have and certain which you should avoid.

The key winning team characteristics tend to be: *balance, leadership, task and target orientation, creative problem-solving ability and positive synergy.*

Let's consider each of these in turn.

▶ *Balance.*

The first and most important consideration should be balance. Long-term winning teams tend to have a spread of abilities and role preferences. The absolute ideal would be an eight-manager team, each with a maximum score on a different preferred role. I have never found one, neither have I been able to create one. I have got very near on a few occasions and each time it proved a winning combination. You should look to balance your team as far as you can but try to do this in an evolutionary rather than revolutionary way. Do not fire people and then rush out and hire replacements until you have fully assessed the potential and talents that exist within you own organisation. Remember:

▶ *Developing people into the job is easier than hiring them into the job.*

The work you have done in the previous chapters can be put to good use in this respect.

▶ *Leadership.*

The next consideration should be management-team leadership. Chairman and Shaper are the two prominent leadership roles; in my experience, if the qualities of both are lacking a winning combination rarely results. Shapers, however, as you may have already gathered from reading the descriptions, are best in ones. Even as few as two Shapers in a team can be disruptive and they can spend all their energy cancelling each other out. Male–female Shaper situations are particularly problematical. If you have a talented Shaper on the team you are leading, keep them fully stretched; you should also make sure their contributions are well-recognised. The day will come, however, when they will need more than just hard work and recognition and that will be the day when you have to decide whether their talents are worth keeping and what the cost of doing so might be.

TOO MANY CHIEFS, NOT ENOUGH INDIANS

I found one unusual and innovative way to deal with too many leaders when I was researching management training needs in the UK. I visited a company following up a research questionnaire only to find it was just one man and two secretaries. Given the grand title of the business, its impressive notepaper and comprehensive response to my questionnaire, I was very disappointed. My disappointment, however, was soon replaced by avid interest as the man explained to me his background and business operations.

The MD of this company had served an apprenticeship in the printing industry and during his time in that industry he had witnessed a variety of industrial disputes and labour problems. When he started his own business he decided he would not allow such problems to occur in any business he owned. As his business started to grow he found that the people who had worked alongside him and whom he had chosen as leaders started to cause problems. His senior managers just could not work well together and spent too much of their energy in fighting. Although he didn't know it he had been recruiting ambitious leader-types, people in fact with similar characteristics to himself, and he had recruited too many of them.

To solve the problem he picked three groups of three managers who could work with each other and set each group up as directors of separate companies. He did this by splitting up the original company and establishing each new company so that it specialised in a different aspect of the original business. It worked like a charm: each new company, with its own talented leader and support team, prospered and grew until in turn it started to get big and experience problems. When this occurred he simply split the companies again. Naturally he started to run out of different existing product splits so he then looked at the special needs of the group's customers and started offering new products into the same or similar markets. He ran his whole operation on four basic principles:

(1) Never let any one company employ more than forty staff.
(2) Never let any one company have a management team larger than four.
(3) Never service or supply more than 10% of a product market and make sure that is the top segment.
(4) Never supply products that sell on price, always sell products on service.

He had 16 successful companies when I visited him. To control the separate companies he never allowed all the directors to meet together. Instead he visited each company in turn and acted as an advisor to each small management team. Each company had to reach targets and work to policies that were jointly agreed and each one had to pay the holding company a services fee and a group development fee each month. Managing the holding company in this way was straightforward and allowed him to move towards the millionnaire bracket.

The moral of the story is simple. Most talented leader-types like to control things rather than be controlled. Controlling them in the traditional manner reduces their contribution potential to the organisation and can threaten it. Don't use traditional control methods to restrict the contributions of talented staff. Find an outlet for their talents that benefits the organisation.

LEADERSHIP AND THE PREFERRED TEAM ROLES

If you are the established leader of your management team, you probably already know that you prefer the Shaper or the Chairman role. If, however, you are a Plant like me you probably think you are or would make a very good leader. I am sorry to tell you that Plants rarely make good leaders, for without training and development they tend to be too selfish and prone to moodiness.

In practice, of course, management-team leaders can come from any of the preferred team role profiles. They will almost certainly already be leading an organisational function team. Generally the people who reach leadership positions do so because they want to be in charge; that desire is, to a greater or lesser extent, a product of their personality. The personality characteristics of the Chairman are, in my opinion, best suited to leading a management team. Management teams need leadership that is level-headed. Shapers, the other main leadership alternative, are too inclined to lose theirs.

If you are in a leadership position and find that you lack some of the qualities the task requires, don't worry: I have devoted a whole chapter to developing leadership skills. As a final point on leadership at this stage, remember:

▶ *Some of the best leaders are those who have leadership thrust upon them.*

▶ *Task and target orientation.*

Management teams must have a disciplined approach to carrying out the organisation's tasks and meeting its targets. This discipline is often generated by those preferring the Completer and Company Worker roles on the management team.

It is the management team that must decide the direction of the organisation. Deciding the direction is, however, only the first task for the team. Someone has to ensure the team fulfils the tasks necessary to keep the organisation moving towards its targets.

Those with the vision to decide organisational goals and targets sometimes lack the ability to cope with the day-to-day practicalities of target achievement. This is where a balanced team will benefit from the contributions Completer and Company Worker managers are able to make. If your team lacks the attributes associated with these two roles the onus is on you as leader to see that it does not spend all its time dreaming up grand plans. Although management teams can succeed without Completers and Company Workers, in my experience they only do so if everyone on the team fully appreciates the need for the discipline they naturally provide. Remember:

▶ *A goal is only a goal when the team scores it.*

▶ *Creative problem-solving ability.*

The operating environment for most organisations gets more complex and competitive as the organisation expands. The raw energy and drive which is often a feature of the management of recently formed organisations will not alone be enough to see most organisations through later stages of development. Managements initially concerned with basic survival subsequently have to make decisions involving changes of direction, expansion, and diversification, as well as taking governmental and international aspects into account. Creativity in product development, market approaches and production methods also become issues. The management team has to have more than just courage: it has to have brains.

If your organisation is growing and is working in a highly competitive environment then you need a highly intelligent Plant on your management team. Plants are like Shapers: best in ones, although they can work together under the right leadership. Plants are also hard to come by. If you don't have one on your team then you should put 'MAC' and 'MATE' to work to help you find one. Very high scores on 'MAC' and 'MATE' will confirm that you are dealing with a Plant. If a 16PF assessment reveals no adverse characteristics such as emotional instability, threat-sensitivity and/or a total lack of discipline, then all you have to decide is whether you and your team can live with this individual.

Management teams can succeed without a Plant but usually only by borrowing ideas. Many management consultants are, by personality, Plants. Using a management consultant to provide an extra input to your management team is an expensive but often highly successful move. You have the added luxury of being able to dispense with their services whenever it suits you without disrupting the management team.

If you have a Plant on your team you have probably already experienced both the benefits and disadvantages they can offer. A strong innovative disposition and an effective thinking ability of a high order are considerable assets to any management team but they must be managed with great skill if negative side-effects are to be avoided. There may, for example, be long periods of non- or low contribution. The Plant is a talented midfield player who is always one step ahead of the others. Once your team learns to match the Plant's attributes with its collective efforts and stops demanding a continuous work rate, you are on your way to success.

▶ Positive synergy.

This whole chapter has been concerned with team work. The concept of 'wa' and the benefits of collective effort have been constantly stressed. Despite the obvious benefits of being a team member, many western managers still treat management-team membership as secondary to functional team leadership. The reason for this is that some managers prefer to be a big fish in a small pond than a rare fish in a large ocean. If your organisation is truly to succeed, it has to overcome this obstacle. If you have a manager whose preferred role is Team Worker then you will have an ally.

You must make management-team membership the most important job in your organisation. If you don't, then you may have to run your organisation on your own. Many entrepreneurs that start to expand their business revert to this approach after finding a management team too difficult to handle. Sadly, most of them will eventually make a major wrong decision, mainly because a lack of team input, and their businesses fail.

Whenever you find yourself struggling with the leadership of your management team remind yourself that you are not infallible and then enlist the help of your Team Worker to get the team back on course.

Chapter Summary

If you have worked your way straight through from Chapter One you probably found the Chapter Four formalised and consolidated both your and your managers' team effort in the quest for greater managerial effectiveness. The reason for this is simple: from the start the processes in the book have encouraged a team outlook and approach. By working through the book as a team you have each already experienced the benefits of a team approach to management.

So what should you and your managers have learnt from tackling Chapter Four? Well you should all now know how the team fits together, where there are overlaps in roles that need modifying and what team parts are missing for a winning combination. You should also know how to use each management team member best in team situations.

If this is so you have made considerable strides in creating not only 'hands on' managers but a 'hands on' management team.

When you are satisfied with your progress in management team development you should move on to Chapter Five. You will then be able to consider how to adapt the structure of your organisation to maximise your management team's chances of success.

5

STRATEGIES, STRUCTURES AND SYSTEMS

The planned approach of this book has enabled you to put into place two long-term success cornerstones for your organisation. One: a team of managers who are really starting to capitalise on their own potential for greater managerial effectiveness. Two: the beginnings of a cohesive, achievement-oriented management team, not just a group of talented individuals.

Chapter Five will help you install another cornerstone: the flexible organisation structures and systems needed for your organisation to operate at its maximum potential. To put this cornerstone in place requires you and your managers to think through and plan for your organisation's future. In other words, to think strategically about where your organisation is going.

During the course of this chapter, you and your management team will be asked to decide your overall strategic goals and targets. You will also be asked to make decisions about your strategic outlook and direction, collectively viewing the role and place of your organisation in its operating environment. This will guide your team as it seeks to achieve goals and targets and enable you together to:

(1) Plan for consistent organisational responses to problems occurring in your operating environment.
(2) Select the resources, both technical and human, that will be needed by the organisation to carry out its role and achieve goals and targets.

Once you have made these strategic decisions you and your management team will be in a position to build flexible structures and systems. That is, structures and systems appropriate for the organisation at different stages of its development.

At the end of this chapter both you and your managers will know where you are taking the organisation, for what purpose, and by what means. You will also have installed the flexible structures and systems needed to support and action your decisions. By completing these processes you will have achieved the following objective.

▶ *The creation of a 'hands on' organisation structure and management system.*

THE NEED FOR ORGANISATION

Most textbooks on management or organisation define 'organisation'. I would define 'organisation' as:

▶*A single word covering the purpose, order, rules and structure of relationships needed to enable a group of people to co-exist with each other, and other groups of people, successfully, so as to try to achieve common or shared goals.*

Let me develop the definition further. All human beings try to order the environment around them. It is natural, therefore, that when they collect together for a common purpose, they will try to organise, that is, structure, the way they operate as a group in the common environment. It is the way they organise both themselves and the things they collectively need, that largely decides whether or not they succeed in achieving their common goals.

Make no mistake about it, to harness collective human energy and use technical resources to maximum effect requires common purpose, order, methods of operating, rules and the establishment of formalised relationships.

Making sure that these purposes, methods, rules and relationships are the right ones and that they work properly is managing. Some managements make the rules, decide the methods and impose relationships and structures with little regard to relevance or purpose. They do so in the belief that managers must manage and that their right to do so must be exercised. Managers do not have the rights to manage for its own sake. Managing is a responsibility to act in the best interests of the organisation as a whole; to organise events and processes so that the organisation can achieve its objectives; and to see that the individuals in the organisation can behave effectively and positively. Imposing rules just to control without purpose is worse than bad management. It is non-management.

A STRUCTURE FOR RELATIONSHIPS

The relationships in an organisation can enable or disable the organisation in its quest for defined targets, objectives and goals. It is management's job to see that they always enable. The manager's main vehicles for this are the organisation's structures and systems. In recent years formal organisation structures and systems have been complicated by management scientists and down-graded by management behaviourists. Sooner or later, when you want to know who does what, where and why, someone gets out an organisation chart. The organisation chart is an indication of a good or bad organisation. How well the relationships on the chart work in reality is an indication of good or bad management.

Of course the need for specific relationships in an organisation will change with the changing purposes, role and direction of the organisation. Relationships also change when the organisation's technology changes; in recent years changes in this area have been both dramatic and far-reaching.

One thing, however, remains constant. As management decides the purpose, role, direction and technology of the organisation, management must also be responsible for structuring the relationships and systems within the organisation. For these planned relationships and systems to be effective, they must relate to the purposes, role and goals of the organisation. Remember:

▶ *An organisation can only be effective if the people in it can act effectively.*

Even when you have successfully installed good structures and systems, it is necessary constantly to review the interaction between purpose and relationships to maintain relevance and effectiveness. In my experience many managements find this difficult. They either change too little too late, or too much too soon. This is, to some extent, understandable. After all managers are also people and can feel threatened by change.

The best structures and systems are usually the ones that everyone can understand and agree. That always means:

▶ *Keep it simple and keep it flexible.*

When I see managers developing giant organisation manuals and complex matrix charts my eyes start to glaze over. People usually ignore over-complex structures and systems and evolve informal working relationships of their own. These mixed official/unofficial relationships and systems usually end up reducing organisational effectiveness. Worse things occur when people try to make complex systems work and get it wrong. They lose their sense of common purpose with the organisation's objectives and end up reducing their contribution to the minimum. Trouble also occurs when complex structures and systems are forcibly imposed. People naturally resist and spend valuable time and energy fighting the 'system'. Only your competitors will win these 'system' battles.

It's always worthwhile to ask your managers to spend time and energy on getting people to understand and agree to how they fit into the structure of relationships in your organisation; it will certainly pay dividends. Remember, the increasing competitive pace of business activities makes change a constant factor. If you want your organisation to survive these changes, it can only do so if you have people who are confident enough in the organisation to adapt readily to change. It is the responsibility of your management to develop that confidence.

What is the current situation in your organisation?

DISCOVERY EXERCISE

Formalising your thoughts on relationships.   *Allow 10 minutes.*

Spend 10 minutes writing down your thoughts on the working relationships in your organisation. Highlight potential problem areas for later discussion.

GOALS AND ORGANISATION

What comes first, the organisation's structure and systems or the organisation's goals and targets? In theory, goals and targets always come first. In practice, you will find you have to plan both at the same time. In an operational organisation, rather than an idealised textbook one, you can't ignore the reality of your existing organisation structure, systems, methods, rules and relationships. But remember:

 The danger is making the goals fit the existing organisation rather than making the existing organisation adapt to the new goals. By all means respect what you already have but never make it into a monument to your organisation's downfall.

The answer is straightforward—make sure you develop people whose first commitment is to the organisation's goals and who readily adapt to change—It will make the whole process a great deal easier.

DECIDING STRATEGY: WAYS AND MEANS

We have now reached the point when you and your management team need to put into practice all the skills and team commitments that you have built up so far. Collectively you need to decide what role you want your organisation to perform in its chosen operating environment, what you want it to achieve and how you intend it to achieve it. First you need to review the strategic outlook for the organisation.

STRATEGIC OUTLOOK

Your organisation's strategic outlook is governed by its operating environment, what is happening in that environment and how you and your management team want to respond to those events. Let me provide you with an example.

I once worked as a consultant for an original equipment manufacturer (OEM) supplying the motor industry. At one stage in its life the company had been the largest manufacturer in the world of the equipment it supplied. Its chosen operating environment was the new motor vehicle industry.

The fuel crisis of 1974 had a major effect on the industry's attitudes to economy and accelerated research into better methods of fuel control. The then management of the OEM chose to believe their sales figures rather than the actuality of their operating environment. Unfortunately their huge order books were the result of long-term planning by the motor industry prior to the fuel crisis. They were three-and-a-half years ahead. Instead of properly reviewing the OEM's strategic outlook and realising that things were going to change radically, the management took the profits and speculated in property and land outside the regular activities of the company.

The lack of planned research investment at this time was almost a death blow. The customers, the vehicle manufacturers, anxious to maintain volume, looked to their suppliers for innovations and found them wanting. Rather than wait for 'the penny to drop', they started their own research and eventually their own manufacture. The OEM's business volume declined very, very slowly but inevitably. This was the worst thing that could happen. The OEM continued to behave as market leader and blamed world trading conditions generally for each year's marginal loss of business. It maintained all of its structures and systems and invested nothing in establishing new markets (moving into new operating environments).

Inevitably the business eventually ran into the red and the shareholders, rather late in the day, replaced the management. The new management immediately saw that there was a future for the company in supplying the existing vehicle market with spares and replacements—a new but related operating environment which had always been available and which had a potential base 20 times larger than the new vehicle market. Everything had to be changed in a revolutionary rather than evolutionary way: thousands of people lost their jobs; systems and structures were hastily dismantled; factories were closed; speculative purchases had to be sold at losses. All these things were symptoms of the management's failure to review the company's strategic outlook correctly. But that was not the only management failure.

No strategic outlook also meant no planned strategic goals and objectives; the management had simply taken the figures supplied to them by their customers. Nobody in the organisation had any real involvement in predicting these figures. People inside the organisation felt they had jobs for life and that they would always have an association with these customers. Even when the associations stopped they believed they would start up again.

When I was appointed as a consultant, the structures and systems in this organisation were for business that no longer existed. I had the unfortunate job of closing down whole departments of skilled people who were working on tasks that were no longer needed. As you can imagine it was a sad affair that could easily have been avoided.

The lessons from this tragic story of mis-management are these:

(1) Management must look beyond the current situation and see what futures the organisation can enjoy. If it doesn't it will have to endure futures others impose.
(2) Management must instill purpose via goals and objectives. If it doesn't its people will work to the objectives of others over which management has no influence.
(3) Management must operate through structures and systems that match current operations. If it doesn't tasks will take longer and cost more, with the inevitable results.

TARGETS, OBJECTIVES, GOALS (TOGs)

Deciding targets, objectives and goals for your organisation should be fun: serious fun, but fun. To ensure positive thinking is the norm. You must decide your TOGs in the right atmosphere—A strategy 'retreat'.

THE STRATEGY 'RETREAT'

In my opinion, the best way to decide your TOGs is to send all of your management team away for two days to a comfortable but quiet retreat with a clear brief and let them thrash them out.

To make this approach work you need a catalyst to lead the team, draw out their ideas, keep them to a tight time-schedule and to formalise the process. It is certainly worth investing in a good 'up front' consultant to do this. As your managers, like most good managers, are probably better with the spoken word than the written word, the consultant can also be used to write up the whole exercise.

▶ *Devil's advocate.*

At the end of the two-day strategic retreat, your team should present their proposed strategies to you and you can then act as a devil's advocate. Alternatively you can lead the team yourself, but I strongly advise against this, for it usually stifles contributions and leads to you having far too much of your own way. After two days working hard as a team your managers are going to be hard to budge and you should direct your efforts and energy at fully testing their commitment and resolve.

▶ *Preparation.*

Make no mistake about it, your managers need time away from the day-to-day pressures to be able to think strategically. If you have 'hands on' managers they will have good number twos who back them up and who can run things while they are away, so there is no need for the organisation to suffer. Give your managers at least three to four weeks to think about and prepare for the exercise. This time is needed to enable them to work with their own teams preparing ideas and suggestions.

▶ *Day-to-day benefits.*

The strategy retreat process should, eventually, be built into the management planning and budgeting cycle of your organisation. Doing this will ensure that your managers regard strategic planning as a part of their job. It will also ensure that all the day-to-day decisions your managers make will be subjected to a strategic influence.

▶ *Guidelines.*

Observing the following guidelines will help ensure your management team's strategy retreat has a positive outcome.

(1) All managers must be committed to preparing thoroughly for the exercise. To ensure this happens check each manager's proposals, without comment, before they go away.

(2) All managers must be committed to arriving at a result, that is a set of strategic proposals to which all team members are committed. If this seems unlikely, lock them up until they have and are.

(3) Make sure the activity is a healthy one. Light meals, limited alcohol, and plenty of exercise facilities should be available. It's a simple fact that the 'mind works better when the body feels good'.

(4) Make sure that the team is not disturbed for any reason. Do this by instructing the venue's management not to pass on any calls except from families and then only at lunch-time and in the evening.

DECIDING STRATEGY: CONSIDERATIONS AND DELIBERATIONS

The most important thing to remember, when deciding strategies, is that the task is to define broad strategies rather than get locked into too much detail. At the strategy stage vision and ideas are more important than dotting the i's and crossing the t's. This does not mean that two days a year is all that your managers need to allocate to considering your organisation's long-term outlook, targets and goals. The two days should be used to make final collective decisions and commitments. Before that can take place, your management team will need to have considered the organisation's current and future operating environment, the opportunities existing in it and the influences upon it. And they must constantly have the organisation's changing strengths and weaknesses in focus.

It should be clear from the aforegoing that your organisation needs systems that generate the data that will enable your managers to make strategic decisions. In the past that may have been a hard and complex task; today there is no excuse for it being so. Computer technology which allows an organisation to monitor its activities in relation to its operating environment is now within the reach of even the smallest organisations. Any manager with access to this technology and the information it can generate should also be able to produce well-considered strategic proposals. Unfortunately in between this technology and your managers are data processing people who speak weird languages and who like to complicate matters. The answer is once again straightforward—don't let them. The only way you can do this is to make sure all of your managers are computer-literate.

We shall soon be reaching a stage in competitive business life where there are only two types of poeple: those who can control and use computers and those who are controlled and used by computers. A good microcomputer on a manager's desk, a couple of 'off-the-shelf' software packages, a really good training programme and plenty of practice is all that is needed to put your managers in the driving seat.

If your managers are not computer-literate your business has no long-term future. Don't hesitate, start getting your managers equipped for your organisation's future today.

▶ *Personality and decisions.*

The strategic decisions your managers have to make will be unique to your organisation and will depend a lot on the personality characteristics and dominant skills your management team possesses. The two extremes are high-risk and conservative. If you have a team with a lot of managers with high 'MAC' scores then you are likely to have a high-risk team.

If your team is dominated by managers with low MAC scores, you are likely to have a conservative team. A high-risk team will be more inclined to make decisions which break new ground and change existing processes to capture new markets. A conservative team will be more inclined to make decisions which seek to refine existing processes so that existing market shares can be defended against competition. You need to play your 'devil's advocate' role very well to ensure over-commitment in either direction does not occur.

In reality the most successful organisations devise strategies that allow them to capitalise on the widest number of situations and opportunities. They are rarely pioneers and usually allow competitors to break most of the new ground. While this is happening, however, they develop contingency plans which can get them quickly into the new market once long-term prospects have been established. On entering a market they direct all their resources towards dominating the segments they select, thereby always maximising the financial return to the organisation. IBM is such an organisation.

▶ The agenda for decisions.

Regardless of the personality inclinations of your management team the agenda for their strategy discussions should be based around the following:

(1) What products and services will the organisation sell in the long term, to whom and in what markets?

This will involve consideration of the organisation's future product/ market mix, the segments of markets it wishes to dominate and how it intends to defend its share of those segments.

(2) What processes, technological and human, will the organisation in the long term have to deploy itself or have others supply to provide the products and services it plans to sell?

This will involve consideration of the organisation's future processes. For example should the organisation's technology be dedicated to specific tasks or be flexible to changing tasks? Dedicated technology gives the best production-cost savings while flexible technology adapts best to changing markets. Training and human resources development options, such as whether to train, hire or contract for the skills needed to supply the planned-for products or services, for example, will need to be considered.

(3) What combination of events and actions must management initiate in the long term to bring about a favourable combination of processes

to meet planned product and service targets and goals?

This will involve seeking synergy, usually via an evolutionary rather than a revolutionary adaptation of the organisation's current processes. Remember:

▶ *The most effective way of bringing manpower and resources into line with planned future products and services is through developed commitment; that is, commitment to those future products and services right across the organisation, because strategies only become realities through people.*

(4) A timetable of the sequence of planned management actions needed to enact the agreed strategies.

This will involve every member of the management team considering what the agreed strategies require of them and when. This timetable should itemise the responsibilities that each manager, jointly with the management as a whole, is committed to and should contain *ideal, realistic* and *fallback* dates for each of the planned management actions.

(5) A linked set of targets and goals for products, services and processes with possible achievement dates.

This is the essence of the whole exercise. It involves saying 'This is what we intend to achieve, long-term, by what we are doing'. As deadlines get closer targets will of course change or firm up but that is not the issue. It is the pro-active nature of agreeing these future targets and goals, using the best information currently available about the organisation's proposed and current operating environments, that provides the organisation with a purpose.

Once you and your management team have agreed where the organisation is going and how you would like to get there, you are in a position to look at what support structures and systems are needed. In other words, you are ready to build in the cornerstone structures and systems that will enable you to fulfill your plans; structures and systems that are both ideal for the current situation and easily adaptable to future needs.

A Japanese house is light but capable both of expansion and of withstanding even a major earthquake. This should be your aim rather than a monumental systems structure that will simply weigh your organisation down and prevent it from changing. On page 133 I have itemised eight first steps to achieving an effective organisation structure. You can reproduce the page for your managers as a source of reference. My approach is to build in flexibility; that is, to create a situation where people expect to change teams and responsibilities with changes in the tasks facing the organisation.

The eight steps to designing an effective organisation structure

DEVELOPMENT GUIDE 25

(1) Identify and define   THE ORGANISATION'S STRATEGIC TARGETS, OBJECTIVES AND GOALS (TOGs).

(2) Identify and define   THE MAIN STAGES AND OPERATIONAL OBJECTIVES ON THE WAY TOWARDS ACHIEVING TOGs.

(3) Identify and define   THE FUNCTIONAL AND SPECIALIST ROLES NEEDED TO ACHIEVE OPERATIONAL OBJECTIVES AT EACH STAGE.

(4) Identify and define   THE KEY TASKS AND PERFORMANCE STANDARDS REQUIRED TO FULFIL THE FUNCTIONAL AND SPECIALIST ROLES AT EACH STAGE.

(5) Identify and define   THE PRIMARY SKILLS AND ABILITIES NEEDED TO PERFORM THE KEY TASKS TO THE REQUIRED PERFORMANCE STANDARDS AT EACH STAGE.

(6) Create and develop   A POOL OF INDIVIDUALS WITH THE SKILLS AND ABILITIES NEEDED TO PERFORM THE KEY TASKS TO THE REQUIRED PERFORMANCE STANDARDS.

(7) Construct and assemble   THE FLEXIBLE TEAMS OF INDIVIDUALS NEEDED FOR FUNCTIONAL AND SPECIALIST ACTIVITIES AT STAGE ONE.

(8) Reconstruct and assemble   APPROPRIATE FLEXIBLE TEAMS FOR EACH SUBSEQUENT STAGE.

CORE ACTIVITIES: STABILITY AS WELL AS FLEXIBILITY

Although the 'eight steps' build in the flexibility needed for goal achievement they do not specifically address the problems of stability associated with certain core activities. These activities, in the main, concern external relationships and they include:

(1) The invoicing and debt-collection component of finance.
(2) Procurement in general.
(3) The field sales force and personnel concerned with specialist outside agencies involved in the organisation's marketing effort.

These activities, and others which may be specific to your organisation, are very necessary for satisfactory goal achievement as they link the organisation with enabling groups outside of the organisation's direct control. Too many changes in the personnel involved in these activities can reduce the organisation's effectiveness. For example:

(1) Credit controllers develop relationships with their counterparts in other organisations and with key accounts, which are essential for the maintenance of the organisation's profits and cash flow.
(2) Buyers develop negotiation skills with key suppliers which result in the extra savings and additional credit facilities that give the organisation an operating edge.
(3) Sales personnel build relationships with customers that generate extra business just when it is most needed. Marketing personnel can convey that vital data which will make a promotion a sure-fire success.

When you are reconstructing the functional and specialist components of your organisation you must not ignore the need for a degree of stability as well as flexibility. Do not leave your organisation open to exploitation from outside because you have moved the people 'in the know'. In your quest for synergy, remember:

DON'T THROW OUT THE BABY WITH THE BATH WATER.

SYSTEMS

The systems that evolve in an organisation do so as a result of the managers' perceptions about their role and the roles of those they manage. These perceptions concern the following five factors:

(1) CONTROL *Who should control what, when and how.*

(2) COMMUNICATION *How communications between key people in the organisation should be conducted.*

(3) _DECISION-MAKING_ _Who should decide what, when and how._

(4) _MOTIVATION_ _What is needed to get people to perform and produce the results the organisation's activities require._

(5) _LEADERSHIP_ _Who should direct whom, when and how._

All of these factors can be varied and manipulated by management to suit the individual needs of a particular organisation. In many instances this manipulation is carried out to achieve specific results such as return on capital employed, cost reductions, productivity increases, etc. These results are recognised measures of organisational performance and may also act as indicators of whether management is doing its job properly.

Although _ROCE_ and similar measures are good indicators of an organisation's progress, they do not provide the total picture. These measures are in the main concerned with short-term performance only. For an organisation to remain successful, long-term development has to take place and methods will be needed to measure long-term success.

THE DANGERS OF THE SHORT-TERM VIEW

It is also dangerous only to value management in terms of its ability to achieve short-term results, as these can be misleading. By only deploying systems and policies designed to achieve short-term results, management could be guilty of neglecting its responsibilities towards an organisation's overall well-being. When managerial survival depends on short-term results it will lead to poor organisational development. Proposals requiring a long-term payback period will be rejected as too difficult to justify.

The systems that evolve from a short-term only approach can have a particularly adverse effect on an organisation's human resources: decision-making power is frequently restricted to management; communications tend to be one way—downwards; motivation processes are directed at achieving immediate goals (overtime and piecework or short-time working and layoffs are prevalent); and punitive controls and autocratic leadership are frequently imposed. In general, systems largely dedicated to short-term results disregard the motivations, perceptions and attitudes of the members of an organisation: the very factors that have the most influence on the organisation's long-term stability and prosperity.

Many organisations fail to pay attention to the attitudes, motivations and perceptions of their people because they are difficult to measure objectively and their payback is equally difficult to assess. In other words, having a happy, well-motivated team with good attitudes towards the organisation will not compensate for failure to make budget.

This seems reasonable until the long-term outlook of the organisation is considered. In the last twenty years we have seen in the west that taking the short-term view has been counter-productive. Japanese managements are never measured only on their short-term results but always on their success in realising their long-term targets, objectives and goals. Long-term success cannot be built on short-term results alone. Remember:

THE SHORT-TERM VIEW MEANS LIMITED HORIZONS.

A short-term results orientation normally requires a closed, autocratic style of management. Research suggests that the organisations that direct more effort into establishing the correct long-term attitudes, motivations and perceptions within the organisation are, long-term, the most successful. These organisations are usually those which adopt a more open, participative management style.

Now it may be that an open, participative management system is not right for your organisation. Not all workers want to have a say in the running of the organisation; many in fact prefer to leave the responsibility for such matters squarely on the shoulders of management. However, new technology, higher standards of education and the need for fewer but more skilled workers all favour a more open, participative approach. These new 'thinking workers' are not likely to respond positively, long-term, to a top-down management style. This being the case, sooner or later management will need to involve them in the decisions which affect both their own destiny and that of the organisation. The managerial decision-making process may well derive considerable benefit from the inputs of these 'thinking workers'. Remember:

COMMITMENT ALWAYS STARTS WITH CONTRIBUTION.

Assessing Your Management System

On the following pages you will find development guides for management systems covering four of the five components of effective management: control, communication, decision-making and motivation. Leadership will be considered in the next chapter. I suggest that you ask each of your managers to work through the guides individually, without reference to their peers. First ask them to read through the guides and then give them the instructions which follow the next paragraph. After they have completed the discovery exercise, let each manager see the others' results so that they can compare their responses.

Earlier in this chapter I asked you to write down your feelings about the relationships in your organisation. You can now use this work, when you have your manager's responses to the discovery exercise, to lead a discussion with your team on the effectiveness of your management systems.

INSTRUCTIONS

The development guides you have just read contain details of alternative management systems covering four of the five factors which most management systems are based on. At the bottom of each guide is a scale numbered 1 to 10; low numbers relate to the participative, open systems and high numbers relate to the autocratic, closed systems. For each of the four factors award a score which you think reflects the situation in your organisation. Once you have decided on a score write down briefly what you think are the features of each of the factors in your organisation.

INTEGRATING: STRATEGIES, STRUCTURES AND SYSTEMS

When discussing organisation structure, I recommended that you developed a pool of human resources that would adapt to the organisation's changing operating conditions. The main advantage of this approach is that the organisation always has a structure deployed in the best way for long term goal achievement.

The 'adapting resources to goals' approach also requires that the organisation's management systems be flexible and fully integrated with the organisation's structures and strategies. Your methods of communication, decision-making and day-to-day control are there to make your strategies work through what you have collectively decided is the most suitable structure of relationships at any given time. All three: strategies, structures and systems, must be constantly in step if maximum effectiveness is to be achieved.

If you decide to emphasise flexibility it is essential that your management is at all times 'hands on'. Make no mistake about it, flexibility can easily change into instability. Your management must be aware of this and be ready to inject the stability and confidence needed to keep a flexible system on the rails.

You and your management team must now consider the results of your collective assessment of your management system with the work you have also started on your organisation's strategies and structures. Slowly, but surely, you have to pull together and integrate the strategies, structures, and systems you have decided to adopt. It is important that

Management Systems: Factor-Control

DEVELOPMENT GUIDE 26

System

Open-participative   *Closed-autocratic*

EMPHASIS

Balanced responsibility-based control: participation.

Centralised, top-down control: limited freedom.

FEATURES

Strategic and financial activities controlled centrally. Operational and functional activities, de-centralised control.

All activities at all levels controlled from the top.

Delegation of authority extensive and related directly to responsibility.

Delegation of authority limited with quick return to overt control.

Qualitative and quantitative controls used, i.e. MBO, management audits, performance appraisal, ROCE.

Extensive use of quantitative control data and mechanisms, i.e. ROCE, production and productivity targeting.

Long-term results most important.

Short-term results paramount.

Minimum layers of supervision with self-supervision prominent.

Several layers of supervision. All tasks requiring overt supervision.

RESULTS

Formal self-control structure: quality circles, etc.

Large informal organisational network promoting covert resistance.

Only limited policing activities required to maintain effectiveness.

High level of policing activities needed to maintain effectiveness.

Mutual respect atmosphere.

Them and us atmosphere.

1 ········· 2 ········· 3 ········· 4 ········· 5 ········· 6 ········· 7 ········· 8 ········· 9 ········ 10

Management Systems: Factor-Control

DEVELOPMENT GUIDE 26

System

Open-participative   *Closed-autocratic*

EMPHASIS

Task-oriented: all directions

Line of command downwards.

FEATURES

Information readily available and linked to task responsibility.

Information restricted and linked to status.

Management communications based on spoken and written word, i.e. active small-group meetings, one-to-one interviews, reports, guideline policies.

Management communications mainly based on the written word, i.e. memos, directives, policy documents, passive large-group meetings.

Small grapevine.

Large grapevine.

RESULTS

Reaction to managerial communications mainly positive.

Reaction to managerial communications mainly neutral or negative.

Responses will be active with a confidence to question and exchange views.

Responses will be passive and compliant with a reluctance to question.

Management reactions to workforce communications likely to be responsive and consultative.

Management reactions to workforce communications likely to be limited, reactionary or paternalistic.

Interactions will be frequent and welcome.

Interactions will be infrequent and resisted.

Reliability of communications will be high due to openness.

Reliability of communications will be low owing to lack of two-way communiction.

1········2·········3··········4·········5·········6··········7·········8·········9········10

Management Systems: Factor-Control

DEVELOPMENT GUIDE 26

System

Open-participative   *Closed-autocratic*

EMPHASIS

Integrated, shared: group.   Top-level, restricted: singular.

FEATURES

Skills-, knowledge- and responsibility-based and task-centred.

Line-of-command based and status-centred.

Extensive involvement: staff always consulted on decisions concerned with their work. The right to be consulted jointly agreed.

Limited involvement or consultation; some legal rights based on national norms and legislation.

Contributions to decision processes welcome from any level, acceptance based on specialist knowledge.

Contributions difficult to make. No easy way for those with specialist knowledge to take part unless invited.

Team approach to most problem-solving and decision-making situations.

Little team activity in decision-making.

RESULTS

High level of commitment to decisions. Staff positively motivated towards related tasks.

Low level of commitment to decisions. Decision processes have little positive affect on staff motivation.

Quality of decisions based on the widest possible relevant inputs.

Quality of decisions limited by the abilities of those at the top.

1 ·········· 2 ·········· 3 ·········· 4 ·········· 5 ·········· 6 ·········· 7 ·········· 8 ·········· 9 ········ 10

Management Systems: Factor-Control

DEVELOPMENT GUIDE 26

System

Open-participative   *Closed-autocratic*

EMPHASIS
Mixed financial: encouraging.

Financial: punitive.

FEATURES

Full salary and bonus.

Graded salary and annual increments.

Achievement-based.

Compliance based.

Rewards based an agreed individual performance.

Rewards based on length of service and nationally negotiated norms.

Standards applied are jointly agreed with senior management.

Standards applied are passed down from senior management.

There are many rewards for initiative both financial and non-financial.

Few rewards for initiative.

Mistakes are seen as part of the development process; trust largely replaces rules.

If rules are broken or mistakes are made, punitive action is taken.

Many growth and development opportunities.

Limited growth and development opportunities.

RESULTS

Individual performance will often rise above average.

Individual performance will rarely rise above average.

Growth and a sense of purpose are the prime motivators.

Security is the prime motivator.

1 ·········2 ·········3 ·········4 ·········5 ·········6 ·········7 ·········8 ·········9 ······· 10

you do not jump too far ahead at this point. Remember:

▶ *Evolution works, revolution hurts.*

You will probably need a number of time-out sessions to reach a workable situation. Don't start changing anything until your team is 100% committed to each course of action. Be aware of the personality characteristics, and therefore the role preferences, of each team member. If they begin to get out of step remind them of the negative features of those characteristics. Remember, you are shaping the future of your organisation; it is no time to allow individuals to indulge themselves at the expense of the effectiveness of the team.

On the next couple of pages you will find comments and advice about the key features of a management system. Use the headings to put together your own agenda for your team's deliberations.

MANAGEMENT SYSTEMS: DOS AND DONTS

▶ *Communication.*

The first thing to remember is that too much communication is as bad as too little. In your enthusiasm to keep people in the picture, do not develop complex communication systems that engulf the important with trivia. A good rule is to make communications action-oriented. Your communications system will be more effective if it facilitates rather than simply informs. Remember, trust limits the need for excessive communication. Develop mutual trust and interdependence and you will reduce memos and rear-covering. Unless you want to know what everyone is doing or has done, avoid purpose-designed memo pads or specialist internal stationery. Even better, ban the typing of all internal communications. This will make people talk to each other rather than at each other and about each other. If you want flexibility and the maximum contribution from everyone in the organisation, let people talk to those whom they need to direct, not through a line of command.

▶ *Decision-making.*

Whatever structure and management style you decide on, ensure that the authority to make decisions is complemented by the ability to do so. Generally, if you want people to achieve results, the power to decide things should be invested in those who have the responsibility for those results.

Delegation is an important part of the decision-making process, but time and personnel development are needed before decision-making can be delegated downwards through an organisation. Be careful: decision-making is a burden not all can handle.

Unless you are employing a team of geniuses, the wisdom to make correct decisions comes only from considering and consulting with those who have to action decisions or are affected by them. Remember: some people are better at making decisions than others and some people make better decisions than others. It is the quality of decisions made rather than their quantity that is important.

If you want to maximise inputs to decisions, expand the use of team decision-making, but make sure that you do not create expensive debating societies. The quality of your organisation's decision-making will also be enhanced if your management information system is designed to be easy to use. Again, quality rather than quantity should be the rule and this can be achieved by building in appropriate filters between the raw data and the data needed by management.

Your managers will make better decisions if they have to make fewer decisions, so try to reduce the number of routine decisions they have to make. That means giving people more authority and responsibility for their own work and reducing overt supervision. Finally, but within reason, support the decisions of your managers, even if you think differently; there is more than one way to get results.

▶ *Control.*

The amount of overt control management has to exercise will depend on the quality of the people being managed. The more overt control you need, the higher your management costs will be; this does not necessarily result in a correspondingly increased payback. The trend is to reduce the layers of supervision by developing self-regulation. Unless you want your managers to spend all their time telling people exactly what to do, introduce positive controls that allow people to correct their own actions, rather than be punished for them. This approach will develop confidence, ability and self-control.

In general, control will be made easier, and a lot fairer, by structuring jobs around mutually agreed tasks and performance standards. People like to know how they are doing and how to do it better; that way control becomes a positive motivation force.

Minor problems can be prevented from becoming major problems by building in prompt informative feedback. Where possible use computer technology to provide this control information; it will enable people to see when things are going off course earlier. Using this type of feedback control also de-personalises the control process and makes it a more routine event.

People make mistakes and their actions will need to be controlled but it is unlikely that they will need to be supressed. Too much control reduces rather than increases organisational effectiveness. It causes people to wait for managerial permission to cover their every action. Developing good feedback systems and self-regulation should develop positive attitudes towards the organisation and reduce the need for overt managerial involvement in organisational routines. These systems will free management to concentrate on controlling and guiding the significant actions needed for overall goal achievement. That is the way to increase the organisation's effectiveness.

▶ Motivation and reward.

Whatever reward systems you finally settle on they must be seen to be equal to the effort, energy and ability you require from your people. Their perception of what is equitable will depend on a number of things:

(1) Can they achieve what is asked of them?
(2) Are their abilities fully recognised and properly used?
(3) In the past have similar efforts been adequately rewarded at the appropriate time?
(4) Are the rewards clear and directly related to the effort that will be required?

In short, people will willingly work towards the achievement of organisational goals, if, and only if, they feel their efforts will enable them to fulfil their own goals in life. As both organisational and personal goals are constantly changing, making these associations is not easy. It is, however, a task that management must tackle.

Many reward systems are based on an individual's level within the organisation. It is assumed that rising to certain levels requires the expression of certain abilities. You have to decide if such a system is right for your organisation. If you are planning a flexible organisation structure, such a reward system could be difficult to operate. At the same time you cannot have a situation in which your people's incomes are constantly fluctuating as they change teams and tasks. One solution might be to separate out people's basic financial rewards from the range of other motivators that are available. Growth, development and achievement can all be built into your organisation's reward system. While it is unlikely that all the positions in your organisation can provide such rewards, it is, of course, possible to give extra rewards collectively to teams for special contributions and to all your organisation's people for a significant success. Some companies have developed this to a fine art giving as much as a 50% total earnings bonus, per year, to employees.

Experience tells me that conventional fairness has, at best, only a neutral effect on individual performance. People, by and large, will perform for rewards related to their individual or team contributions, rather than because they have been there for a certain number of years or are graded at a certain level. Grade and service rewards rarely generate any extra performance, but once you build them into the system it is hard to get rid of them. You have to decide whether, long-term, you can afford them.

Spend a lot of time finding the right reward and motivation system for your organisation and don't be afraid to modify it in the light of experience if you need to. Remember, the more you link rewards to individual contributions the more contribution you are likely to generate.

▶ *Summary.*

Communication, decision-making, control, rewards and motivation are all main components of a management system. The significant remaining component is leadership and this is the subject of the next chapter. All of these components must be regarded, along with the structure of relationships in your organisation, as facilitators of the organisation's chosen strategies. They are not, and must never be, treated as ends in themselves.

CHAPTER SUMMARY

We have now reached the penultimate stage in creating the 'hands on' manager. This 'management in action' chapter is designed to help you and your management team exercise the managerial prerogative of deciding your organisation's strategies, structures, and systems.

As a team what should you have gained from this 'management in action' process? I would highlight three key points:

(1) By working your way through Chapter Five you and your management team have been testing, in every sense of the word, your ability to work together as a team. All the tasks in Chapter Five are team-oriented and can only work successfully through committed team-work. If your team's efforts produce a working blueprint for your organisation's future success, you can count that as a major gain for your organisation.

(2) Each member of your team should now have a greater understanding of where your organisation is, where it is going in the future, and the roles they are required to play in enabling it to achieve its goals. If each team member is able to demonstrate a sense of real purpose in fulfilling their organisational role, count that as another major gain.

(3) In designing the structure of relationships and supporting systems needed for implementing your organisation's strategies, your managers will have helped to shape the organisational environment in which they feel they will be most effective. If your managers are now starting to tackle every problem and task as though they have a 'home game advantage', that also is a major benefit.

Finally, remember the processes in Chapter Five are not to be considered in isolation. With modification and adaptation they can be used periodically to maintain the effectiveness of your organisation.

Once you are satisfied that you and your team have come to terms with your organisation's strategies, structures and systems you can move on to the next chapter, leadership.

6

MANAGING LEADERSHIP

Leadership is the least understood subject in management and organisation. 'Managing leadership' enables you and each of your managers to come to terms with the concept of 'managership'; that is, with the use of leadership in a managerial context for organisational advantage.

This chapter will consider leadership, what it is and isn't, how it works and the differences and links between leadership and management. Special emphasis will be placed on developing the managership behaviour of the chief executive. Each of your managers will be asked via a discovery exercise to examine critically their approach to leading and the relative effectiveness of that approach as applied on behalf of your organisation. Examples will be provided of different leader-manager styles and the relative advantages and disadvantages of each style in specific contexts.

The chapter will go on to examine the assumptions managers have about people and how these assumptions affect both leadership and managing. Each of your managers will be asked to assess their own managerial assumptions and consider how these influence their own approach to leader–manager situations.

It is likely that this last chapter will cause both you and your managers to re-examine the values that influence your approach to leading and managing. This may not always be comfortable but it will certainly be worthwhile. By getting this far with developing the 'hands on' manager you and your managers have demonstrated your receptiveness to new approaches and ideas. You now need to capitalise on this receptiveness to achieve the main objective of the chapter:

▶ *The development of stable and effective managership in your organisation.*

MANAGEMENT AND LEADERSHIP

Leadership in organisations does not occur in isolation; it is, if you like, the icing on the management cake. The skills, structures, systems and strategies of management all work better if appropriate leadership is used in their co-ordination and implementation.

All managers, if they are truly managing, should exercise some form of leadership, but management and leadership should not be mistaken for the same thing. For most managers leadership must be regarded as a component of the larger job of managing. Even in the two management positions which require the greatest leadership qualities, the supervisory and chief executive roles, leadership is still only a component of a bigger job.

Make no mistake about it, to be a successful manager requires more than good leadership qualities. It means combining the qualities of leadership with the broader and more comprehensive skills of managing.

To understand how leadership and managing can be combined we first need to look at some of the features and possible effects of leadership.

▶ *The power of the leader.*

The actions people take in response to a leader can bring them both rewards and disappointments but once they decide to follow someone it is difficult to deter them. Leaders seem to have the power to inspire great commitment from people, sometimes commitment which defies logic or reason. This is the leader's great strength and also the leader's Achilles' heel. History is full of leaders who failed when they started to believe in the myth of their own invincibility.

▶ *The promise of the leader.*

One of the reasons leaders inspire people and attract supporters is the promise of success, a better tomorrow, etc. People like to be a part of something successful, something that is going places, something that will improve their lot in life. To offer people more than they already have in return for their support is a common promise made by leaders. Politicians are past masters of this approach. People tend to correlate success with leadership and follow the leaders they think will take them towards success. Equally leaders who become associated with failure find it difficult to retain their supporters. Remember:

▶ *The leader who fails in the end fails to lead.*
▶ *The need to retain leadership.*

Leadership also has a manipulative element. In fact, the ability to manipulate and deploy relationships and systems to the maximum effect is the hallmark of many a successful leader. Machiavelli wrote a famous book on the subject, *The Prince*. In *The Prince*, Machiavelli recommends that leaders should promote dis-harmony amongst those who could challenge their leadership position—a divide-and-rule approach. Unfortunately Machiavelli's Prince eventually fails but only because of circumstances outside his control. I am not convinced by Machiavelli's arguments. Let me give you a modern day example.

I once worked as a consultant for an entrepreneur who had built up a very successful business by acquiring the UK franchises of American products. When he started he knew nothing about accounting so he was forced to take a partner. This partner put money into the business and became a director and major shareholder.

While the entrepreneur was fully occupied getting products from America and then customers in the UK, the business prospered. As the business became bigger, staff were employed and leadership became an issue in the company.

The entrepreneur really believed he had great leadership qualities; he certainly had a charisma that attracted considerable loyalty from his staff. He acted all the time as if he were the sole leader and constantly undermined his partner's authority. He did this even in financial matters, about which he knew very little. He would always deal with his managers on a one-to-one basis. He would pretend to share confidences exclusively with each of them, while at the same time running down the other managers.

The reality was that the business was becoming too big for him to handle and he was getting more an more out of his depth. Of course, what he should have done was to share out the responsibilities more and develop his managers. He was unwilling to do this and did not want to share the leadership of the company with anybody. Instead his approach drove out the good managers and forced him to retain more of the decision-making process. He gave great financial rewards to staff who remained loyal to him and promoted them above their competence. He relied upon his personal charisma to handle every problem, often making promises he could never keep and then blaming others for the inevitable failures.

Eventually things started to go wrong and the bank called in the company overdraft. Even though he was the leader he refused to accept any responsibility for the company's downward spiral, blaming his partner (who did accept the responsibility), his managers and his staff. The crisis only strengthened his belief that he alone had the ability to lead the organisation forward.

I have to admit that even though I spent most of my time in the organisation just repairing the damage caused by his inappropriate behaviour, I really liked this man. He had tremendous self-belief and drive and had to be admired, even though these qualities were taking his organisation in the wrong direction.

During a period of calm after the bank had put on some tight controls, business picked up and profits returned. However, before this improvement could be consolidated he bought a Rolls-Royce. He was convinced that his approach was winning. The business went broke two years later.

▶ *Leader behaviour versus manager behaviour.*

It must be clear from the above that combining leadership with management is no easy task and many managers try to avoid testing or developing that component of their job. These managers rely heavily on the established structure of relationships and systems within the organisation to get results. Leaders, on the other hand, are inclined to sweep away structures and systems to get their own way, sometimes with little regard for the long-term consequences of their actions. Neither approach is in the long-term interests of the organisation. Managers who avoid using the behavourial tools for getting people to do things are rarely able to generate the synergy needed to give their team a winning edge. Leaders who disregard the organisation's structures and systems frequently lead their willing team off in the wrong direction . . . or *over* the edge!

▶ *Leadership transferability.*

Although successful leaders are often unable to identify the foundations of their success, they think they have a transferable asset which will work in all circumstances. This is rarely true. Successful managers on the other hand, usually have a wider range of identifiable skills and abilities developed during the course of managing. These skills and abilities are normally transferable to different job situations and will still produce results. This is the most important difference between management and leadership. One is based on a mix of developed skills and abilities stemming from personality characteristics and the other is based purely on personality characteristics.

Morita, Weinstock and Bond, all of whom we will be discussing shortly, have exercised great power and that has a lot to do with their success. Unfortunately there are not many leaders about who can handle such power. In the entrepreneur example I gave power was not complemented by intellect and failure was the result. Power must be matched with the ability to use it wisely.

Dr An Wang, the founder of Wang Laboratories is another leader of merit. In his autobiography *Lessons*, Wang suggests that chief executives who are able to take their organisations down the wrong path unchecked are eventually brought to heel by outside forces in their operating environments. That is what happened to the entrepreneur in my example. Unfortunately, as Dr Wang also points out, those who are required to lead but who are so controlled that they can only take a short-term view, eventually also fail their organisations. Dr Wang, of course, has proved that it is possible to be a successful leader-manager, over a long time span, with considerable power.

Morita, Weinstock, Bond and Wang all use leadership as a 'capstone' over their management skills. All clearly have different styles and approaches to leadership but they are all successful leader-managers. They still have vision but their use of the power invested in them is only exercised on behalf of their organisations and through highly competent management teams which they themselves developed.

▶ *Managership.*

Leadership is without doubt an emotive subject on which everyone has an opinion. For my part I feel that most organisations would be best served if leadership was considered complementary to management rather than a substitute for it. In other words, managership is the essential element which successful organisations need. It is my experience that most organisations need managers who can lead rather than leaders who think they can manage. That means that the planning, organising and decision-making abilities needed to manage an organisation successful in the long term have to be combined with the leadership qualities of inspiring, motivating and driving people into action.

▶ *Power and leadership.*

Leadership is primarily concerned with power. Those who want to lead do so because they want to exercise power over people and situations. That is their primary motivation. Managers like the responsibility and authority that go with the job but the need to achieve is more important than the desire for power.

It is the stability of the personality of the leader that is the key to the leader's long-term effectiveness. History contains many examples of leaders who eventually became unstable in their responses to situations; leaders like Alexander the Great, Napoleon and Hitler. All these leaders craved power and loved to exercise it. In the business world we also have examples from Robert Owen through to Henry Ford and Steven Jobs. These industrial and business leaders had vision and wanted to change the order of things; to do so they needed power and power is what they sought. Henry Ford exercised so much power in his organisation that when he departed he left a vacuum that nearly broke it. Steven Jobs, one of the founders of Apple, always liked to give the impression that Apple was a democratic company run by a team. In reality he had so much charisma and drive that things revolved very much around him. In 1983, when Apple were going through a difficult period, Jobs brought in a professional manager, John Scully. It is Scully, not Jobs, who now runs Apple.

▶ *Leadership that works.*

There are also many examples of great leader-managers who have been able to harness their leadership qualities to the job of managing. Akio Morita of Sony is a splendid example and the long-term success of Sony is a tribute to his stable managership. Arnold Weinstock is another example: his skilful leadership has managed to weld a group of disjointed companies into GEC and make it work. Alan Bond of the Bond Corporation of Australia is a less obvious example; yet, despite his public image, Bond has built up, and is successfully managing, a very large and highly profitable group of companies.

LEADERSHIP STYLES

What then is an appropriate leadership–managership style? Well, that depends on you, the people you have to lead and the situations and circumstances under which your managership is required. Let's consider these three things in more detail.

▶ *You: the leader-manager.*

Your approach to a leadership situation will be influenced by the dominant characteristics of your personality, the needs you have, your values and inclinations to act in a certain way. For example, if swift progress and action are important to you then you are likely to find a participative style of leadership more difficult to maintain. If you need the affiliation of people then you might be inclined to lead in a way that attracts affiliation.

▶ *Them: those under your leadership-management.*

Your approach to leadership will also be influenced by your perception of how much leadership your people need. You will have a perception of their dependence on you, how much freedom they seek for their actions, what knowledge and skills they want to exercise, what expectations they have. If you see them as lacking in foresight and direction you are likely to try to provide that. If you think that all they need is the right forum to express their skills and knowledge in the best interests of the organisation, you are likely to become the catalystic leader who creates that forum.

▶ *Leadership: situations and circumstances.*

Finally your style has to be right for the situation and circumstances under which you are required to exercise leadership. The more flexible your organisation needs to be to survive, the more your people will need to be consulted and involved, if they are to remain effective contributors.

If your organisation has to react quickly to situations you will have less time for exercising the democratic processes. You will have to be more commanding and tell people what to do. If you need to call upon a pool of expertise to maintain your organisation's effectiveness, your style will need to be more democratic. Experts rarely respond to simple overt direction.

WORKING TOWARDS MANAGERSHIP

Each leadership style has advantages and disadvantages. Wisdom is therefore required in the selection, adaptation and use of a leadership style. To help you and your managers think about your own approach to leadership and work towards a managership approach, I have devised a simple discovery exercise which I would suggest you and your managers now undertake. The exercise is laid out so you can reproduce it.

DISCOVERY EXERCISE

Managership Part One.   *Allow 25 minutes.*

When you and each of your managers have drawn your leadership profiles discuss and compare them. The important thing to remember when doing this is:

▶ *There is no one right style and approach but there are inappropriate styles and approaches.*

Every style and approach has advantages and disadvantages which will be discussed later in the chapter.

What is also important is the accuracy of each manager's perception of how they lead. The procedure for assessing this makes up Part Two of the discovery exercise; you will find the details for this have been included after the set of statements.

DISCOVERY EXERCISE

Managership Part Two and feedback discussion.   *Allow 25 minutes.*

You can check the accuracy of your managers' perception of how they lead by issuing sets of the statements to the members of the teams of each of your managers, with the following introduction:

Below there are 20 statements made by leaders of teams. Under each statement you will find a scale running from 1 to 10. Consider the statement in relation to how you feel about the way you are led. If

Working towards 'Managership'

DEVELOPMENT GUIDE 27

STATEMENTS

Below are listed 20 statements made by leaders of teams. Under each statement you will find a scale running from 1 to 10. Consider the statement in relation to how you feel about the way you lead your team. If you feel that you could make a similar statement about your own situation choose a high point on the scale. The more the statement fits your approach the higher the point you should choose. If you feel that you couldn't really make such a statement about your own situation choose a low point on the scale. The less the statement fits your approach the lower the point you should choose.

(1) When my team are gathered together informally to solve a problem I usually take the initiative and direct the way the discussions go.

1 ········2 ·········3 ·········4 ·········5 ·········6 ·········7 ·········8 ·········9 ·········10 ········

(2) It is my job to maximise my team's efforts. I like to set targets and deadlines and expect my team to comply with them. They know I mean business and everyone knows where they stand.

1 ········2 ·········3 ·········4 ·········5 ·········6 ·········7 ·········8 ·········9 ·········10 ········

(3) My team look to me to solve the problems and I encourage them to bring their problems to me. That way I can control progress and keep the team working well.

1 ········2 ·········3 ·········4 ·········5 ·········6 ·········7 ·········8 ·········9 ·········10 ········

(4) I communicate with my team in an open and frank way and expect the same from them. At first some people don't like what I have to tell them but I make sure they agree.

1 ········2 ·········3 ·········4 ·········5 ·········6 ·········7 ·········8 ·········9 ·········10 ········

(5) Giving people authority to do things is a two-way exercise. Before I give any of my team authority to do anything they have to prove they are responsible enough to do it.

1 ········2 ·········3 ·········4 ·········5 ·········6 ·········7 ·········8 ·········9 ·········10 ········

(6) I have the ideas and know which way to go. People have a choice when they join my team. Join a winning team and accept my leadership or join the also-rans and debate things.

1 ········2 ·········3 ·········4 ·········5 ·········6 ·········7 ·········8 ·········9 ·········10 ········

(7) The team is the most important part of the equation. The results we get stem from developing our working relationships. I am the leader but I respect everyone's input.

1 ········2 ·········3 ·········4 ·········5 ·········6 ·········7 ·········8 ·········9 ·········10 ········

(8) It's no good me setting unrealistic targets for my team or spending too much time agreeing targets with them. The nature of our work is complex; I set the parameters and they get on with it. I only hear from them when they need my advice.

1 ········2 ·········3 ·········4 ·········5 ·········6 ·········7 ·········8 ·········9 ·········10 ········

(9) It's really a question of balance. If I think the majority of the team want to go in that direction and that those who don't won't object too much, I let the majority run with the ball. It works.

1 ········2 ·········3 ·········4 ·········5 ·········6 ·········7 ·········8 ·········9 ·········10 ········

(10) You can't get anywhere without rules and procedures. I tell everyone the rules and then expect them to follow them. If they don't then eventually we have to bring them into line. This is a happy team here. Everyone knows what is expected of them.

1 ········2 ·········3 ·········4 ·········5 ·········6 ·········7 ·········8 ·········9 ·········10 ········

Working towards 'Managership'

DEVELOPMENT GUIDE 27

(11) I never cease to be amazed by the contributions people come up with in team meetings. Our progress is attributable to the way we get people to contribute their ideas on problems.

1 ·········2 ·········3 ·········4 ·········5 ·········6 ·········7 ·········8 ·········9 ·········10 ········

(12) Everyone in the team is a specialist. Each works on set projects with set budgets. I provide direction and guidance and interpret corporate strategies and thinking. I see my job as pulling the whole thing together when the time is right.

1 ·········2 ·········3 ·········4 ·········5 ·········6 ·········7 ·········8 ·········9 ·········10 ········

(13) From the beginning we realised that we had to operate with policies and procedures. Handling the personal finances of people is a tricky business. Everybody in my team knows exactly how they should respond in a given situation.

1 ·········2 ·········3 ·········4 ·········5 ·········6 ·········7 ·········8 ·········9 ·········10 ········

(14) Of course my people know that they can see me anytime if they have a problem. My policy has always been to have an open office door. I am confident that I can count on their support and I meet regularly with them to discuss the future.

1 ·········2 ·········3 ·········4 ·········5 ·········6 ·········7 ·········8 ·········9 ·········10 ········

(15) The team is highly motivated. They want to know what has to be done and hear my views on how they should proceed. Once the direction has been established I let them get on with it. Sometimes things go wrong but all in all it works well.

1 ·········2 ·········3 ·········4 ·········5 ·········6 ·········7 ·········8 ·········9 ·········10 ········

(16) Thousands of people work in this place and their efforts have to be marshalled and controlled. So that everyone knows where they are we have set up operating procedures and working relationships. As long as people stick to these there are no real problems.

1 ·········2 ·········3 ·········4 ·········5 ·········6 ·········7 ·········8 ·········9 ·········10 ········

(17) When I came here it was a small independent office and everyone knew everyone else's first name. It soon became clear that we could not maintain that atmosphere and remain effective. It's sad but now I only know most people by their extension number.

1 ·········2 ·········3 ·········4 ·········5 ·········6 ·········7 ·········8 ·········9 ·········10 ········

(18) Working with people is important to me. I like to have happy people around me. I 'walk the floor' every day and keep people up to date on things. My style is to keep people informed; that way they learn to trust my leadership.

1 ·········2 ·········3 ·········4 ·········5 ·········6 ·········7 ·········8 ·········9 ·········10 ········

(19) When I need the support of the work team, I ask for it. Sometimes I have to lay it on the line but in general they like the way I deal with them. They know I listen.

1 ·········2 ·········3 ·········4 ·········5 ·········6 ·········7 ·········8 ·········9 ·········10 ········

(20) I really take a back seat as far as my team is concerned. When they need my advice or help they know where to come but that is unusual. My prime function is to bridge the gap between them and senior management.

1 ·········2 ·········3 ·········4 ·········5 ·········6 ·········7 ·········8 ·········9 ·········10 ········

you feel that your leader could make a similar statement choose a high point on the scale. The more the statement fits your leader's approach the higher the point you should choose. If you feel that your leader couldn't really make such a statement choose a low point on the scale. The less the statement fits your leader's approach the lower the point you should choose.

Ask the team members to complete the statements on their own, in confidence and without any need to identify themselves. They may then return them to you for your analysis or, if your organisation is really democratic, discuss their views and submit composite team profiles to their managers.

Comparing a person's perception about themselves with how others see them can be very revealing and if good relations exist between the parties, good fun. However, take care not to create any friction between your managers and their teams. For the best results, try to approach the whole exercise in a positive but light-hearted manner. If the results are at odds then get the parties to look at the differences together. This approach should help enhance effective leadership in your organisation.

STYLES AND APPROACHES: ADVANTAGES AND WEAKNESSES

Instantly commanding respect and obedience; overtly directing and controlling people's actions; purposefully sweeping aside all opposition in the quest to complete their mission. Sounds like the behaviour of everyone's stereotype leader doesn't it? In fact most people regard such strong, forthright behaviour as leadership and when individuals are appointed to leadership positions they often try to behave in such a way. For some it works, but for many if doesn't, they just become ineffective bullies demanding rather than earning the respect of their people.

The autocratic style and approach to leadership is probably the one that is closest to the stereotype image of leadership and is the one we will look at first.

AUTOCRATIC

The base for this approach is authority, the authority to tell people what to do and demand that they do it. The authority may come from knowledge, position or the power to reward and punish. It does not matter, wherever it comes from it will be used like a club. Autocratic leaders expect to receive unquestioning obedience: they know what is best and that is that. Of course, sometimes they are right about things

Working towards 'Managership'

DEVELOPMENT GUIDE 27

SCORESHEET

You can now plot your approach to leadership situations on the following chart. The process is simple: ring the score for each question on the vertical line related to the question and then join the rings across.

The stars under the statement question numbers indicate the weight (importance) of the statement in relation to the leadership approach the statement represents.

The numbers under the stars indicate what would be an appropriate 'managership' score for that particular leadership approach.

Free rein	Participative	Diplomatic	Bureaucratic	Autocratic
10 10 10 10	10 10 10 10	10 10 10 10	10 10 10 10	10 10 10 10
9 9 9 9	9 9 9 9	9 9 9 9	9 9 9 9	9 9 9 9
8 8 8 8	8 8 8 8	8 8 8 8	8 8 8 8	8 8 8 8
7 7 7 7	7 7 7 7	7 7 7 7	7 7 7 7	7 7 7 7
6 6 6 6	6 6 6 6	6 6 6 6	6 6 6 6	6 6 6 6
5 5 5 5	5 5 5 5	5 5 5 5	5 5 5 5	5 5 5 5
4 4 4 4	4 4 4 4	4 4 4 4	4 4 4 4	4 4 4 4
3 3 3 3	3 3 3 3	3 3 3 3	3 3 3 3	3 3 3 3
2 2 2 2	2 2 2 2	2 2 2 2	2 2 2 2	2 2 2 2
1 1 1 1	1 1 1 1	1 1 1 1	1 1 1 1	1 1 1 1

STATEMENTS

Free rein	Participative	Diplomatic	Bureaucratic	Autocratic
8 12 15 20	7 9 11 14	1 4 18 19	10 13 16 17	2 3 5 6

WEIGHT OF THE STATEMENT IN RELATION TO THE APPROACH

Free rein	Participative	Diplomatic	Bureaucratic	Autocratic
* * * *	* * * *	* * * *	* * * *	* * * *
* * * *	* * *	* * * *	* * *	* * * *
* * * *	* *	* * *	* * *	* * *
* * * *	* *	* * *	* * *	*
* * * *	*	*	* * *	*

MANAGERSHIP SCORES

Free rein	Participative	Diplomatic	Bureaucratic	Autocratic
6 8 9 6	6 8 5 4	4 7 3 8	5 9 6 1	8 6 4 3

and their approach is right for the situation. Used with skill, the autocratic style can galvanise people into action and achieve almost instant results. In a crisis or emergency situation it is often necessary for someone to take total command of the situation. Equally, in such situations people respond willingly, relieved that someone is handling the problem at last. Long-term, the exclusive use of this approach is doomed to failure.

It is unlikely in a modern organisation that one person can make all the right decisions all the time. If autocratic leaders put themselves in that position, sooner or later expensive mistakes and misunderstandings occur. Even the autocratic leader whose approach is more paternalistic usually finds it difficult to listen to the advice of others. They pretend to be open and receptive but once their ideas are challenged they show their true colours.

▶ *Managership and the autocratic approach.*

Managership sometimes requires that a manager takes total and unquestioning command of an event or situation. In really effective and efficient organisations such events and situations should be few and far between.

BUREAUCRATIC

If everyone knows the rules and how to interpret them then the organisation will have little need for overt autocratic behaviour. Sounds good doesn't it? Well, that is the dream behind the bureaucratic approach to leadership. Bureaucracy is based on fairness not inefficiency, but you would hardly think so when it comes to dealing with bureaucracy and those who act as leaders in bureaucratic organisations. Remember:

▶ *The trouble with de-personalising human relations is that people get in the way.*

It's not possible to remove human judgement from organisational behaviour and decision-making. But this is just what the predominantly bureaucratic leadership approach tries to do. Don't misunderstand me: rules, regulations and procedures are essential to all organisations that want to operate effectively. This is particularly true in organisations that have a special trust relationship with their clients—banks, insurance companies, policing, etc. Even in these organisations administering rules without purpose or reason must be regarded as counterproductive.

The missing ingredient in many bureaucracies is human judgement. Bureaucratic leaders do not have the overt fire and single-minded belief of the autocrat; they have a book of rules instead. The rules are the main base for the leader's approach: once invested with the authority to see the rules are carried out, these leaders often set about the task with the zeal of a hanging judge. 'No exception' is the order of the day.

In the end, unless these organisations are operating in a protected environment, such a leadership approach is bound to fail. The pace of most operating environments is too fast for the exclusive use of the bureaucratic leadership approach. Today's leader-managers have to be prepared to adapt and change things if their organisations, and they themselves, are not to be overtaken by events.

An example of the problems of bureaucratic leadership can be found in China. The Chinese are trying to improve and open up their economy but their attempts are running into serious problems. Western organisations are going into China hoping to do good business in a rapidly expanding market. Nearly all of the organisations that I have spoken to are disappointed with the results. The problem is always the same—red tape. Western management techniques have run headlong into entrenched bureaucratic practices and leadership and these have proved to be much bigger stumbling blocks than lack of investment and skills put together. The Chinese leader-managers have, over many years, turned the means—rules, regulations and procedures—into an art form and they are unable to dismantle it easily.

▶ *Managership and the bureaucratic approach.*

Managership requires that due respect be given to the organisation's rules, regulations and procedures. It will use, not abuse, the structure of relationships in an organisation. This does not mean that these things should be supported for their own sake. Acting to maintain the highest level of contribution from people is managership in action.

DIPLOMATIC

The dangers both of an exclusively autocratic and an exclusively bureaucratic approach to leadership are obvious and can be easily spotted. The pitfalls of the diplomatic approach are less clear, especially to the leader/manager who practises them.

Diplomats think they are democrats; in fact most of the managers I know who use the diplomatic approach do so in the belief that they are highly participative. At best this approach is skilful manipulation; at worst it is paternalistic.

The diplomatic approach does have a place in areas where the people on the receiving end are in 'go-nowhere' but important jobs. These people are usually aware of the limitations of their positions but do not like to be constantly reminded of it by thoughtless autocrats or bureaucrats. A skilful diplomatic approach can keep these people happy and contributing.

I have to admit that I do use this approach from time to time and have found it extremely successful; I do make sure, however, that I know who I am dealing with before I use it. The secret of successful diplomatic leadership is consistency. The leader who forgets this is lost and will be regarded just as an insincere manipulator. The other danger is that a diplomatic approach can be taken by some as a sign of weakness, so authority has to show through if loss of respect is not to occur. If you decide to use the diplomatic approach make sure you can win your people over most of the time. You need to be a very good salesperson.

▶ *Managership and the diplomatic approach.*

Managership recognises that not all the people in the organisation have the same clear perception of direction as their leaders. People sometimes have to be sold new ideas and solutions. There is nothing wrong with this as long as those people are given the courtesy and follow-up a first-class professional salesperson would give to a client. The diplomatic approach, if used wisely, will convince and commit people; but it must not be over-used. Over-use and lack of sincerity turns diplomats into wheeler-dealers that nobody trusts.

PARTICIPATIVE

Participation increases performance but participation only works when the people taking part also accept the responsibilities of participation. The environment in which participation is to take place must be properly prepared; that preparation is the responsibility of the leader-manager who wishes to use a participative approach. A participative leadership style can take up a great deal of a manager's time; if used inappropriately this time will largely be wasted. Remember:

▶ *There is a marked difference between planned delegation and abdication.*

If you intend to be predominately a participative leader-manager then there are two essentials: responsibility and skill.

Not all people want to participate and be involved in the running of their organisation and not all people have the skills and abilities to be able to do so, even if they wanted to. First, make sure your people can and want to handle the responsibility that true participation demands. Then make sure your people are skilled enough to put forward ideas that you are more than likely to act upon. Nothing weakens the desire to participate actively more than having one's ideas constantly rejected.

Human motivation being what it is, if you are a participative leader-manager, you will have a more than even chance of getting a payback from a planned participative approach. Most people like recognition and to feel that their contributions are important, they like to experience achievement and be part of a success. With care you can have these personal motivation factors built in and working for you.

Participation can take the form of total democracy or considered consultation. Being a total democrat is hard for most leader-managers as they feel it leaves them too open to the wishes and demands of the majority.

▶ Democratic participation.

Democratic participation, whereby staff are able to participate democratically in the running of the organisation, albeit on a limited basis, can be a successful alternative to total democracy. The John Lewis Partnership have practised this form of democratic leadership for years with great success. Staff meet once a week with management and express their views and wishes on the running of their department. Rank is not a consideration at these meetings. Management is required to explore the ideas and suggestions made and report back to the members or the partners, as the staff are known within the company. Over the years that I have visited and observed John Lewis's managers and staff I have never encountered any outstanding manager-leaders; that is, individuals with great vision striving to achieve difficult goals via some grand plan. What I have found is an environment in which a collective approach really works. An inspection of John Lewis's track record over the last forty years will confirm this.

Adopting a consultation form of participative leadership will allow the leader-manager to retain final decision-making authority and thereby avoid the problems associated with total democracy. This approach requires great skill if it is to be effective. Genuine consultation and involvement must not only take place but must be seen to take place. All the pros and cons of each individual idea and argument must be explored. The whole process can be very time-consuming and not all leader-managers have the necessary patience. If you plan to use this approach, make sure you are able to sustain it.

Even after the actual consultation process has been completed it is still necessary to deal carefully with those whose ideas were not taken up. To remain effective, the participative-consultative leader has to retain the goodwill of everyone, winners and losers, and ensure they continue to make positive contributions.

▶ *Managership and the participative approach.*

Managership recognises all the benefits of participation but is realistic when trying to capitalise on their application. Both the main types of participative leadership—democratic and consultative—need the right operating environment if they are to succeed. Managership involves setting up the best environmental conditions for effectiveness regardless of the leadership approach adopted.

FREE-REIN

In some situations any form of overt leadership is greatly resented. Highly specialised personnel with very specific and important tasks to perform usually have a strong dislike of being managed or lead.

Doctors, architects, lawyers, consulting engineers and other highly qualified specialists just cannot be controlled and dealt with in the same way as shop-floor production workers. There have been times when I wished they could. Despite their obvious worth and intelligence, these specialists tend to lack the collective purpose and vision needed to make the organisations they belong to work effectively. Not to put too fine a point on it, they are often downright selfish. Normally the only way these much-needed individualists can be led and managed is via a laissez-faire approach.

There are, of course, many advantages in using a laissez-faire/free rein style with highly intelligent workers but the dangers are also very great. The secret of the successful application of a predominately laissez-faire approach lies in having a total understanding of what makes these individuals tick. Remember people can only be given this type of freedom if they have a high level of competence and the integrity to use it wisely. If you intend or find you have to concentrate on this leadership approach then be sure you know all of your people's strengths and weaknesses and that they have the right level of competence and integrity that will enable a laissez-faire approach to work.

▶ *Freedom by sticking to the rules.*

One way to keep these specialists working in the right direction is to lay down rules for the continuation of their freedom. I call this FSR, 'freedom by sticking to the rules'. It usually works if you make sure you get the rules right. Remember, the cleverer the people you have to lead, the more likely they are to find loopholes in your approach to leading and managing them. Budgets, resource allocations, completion dates, one-to-one interviews and other traditional control methods can be used for managing the performance of these specialists, but be sure they do not include any ambiguity or open-ended standards.

The need for mutual respect.

When it really comes down to it, the best way to lead specialists is by mutual respect. This usually has to be earned on both sides; the leader must take the initiative. This does not mean pandering to the demands of specialists because your organisation must have their skills. It does mean listening to their requirements and demonstrating an understanding of what they are trying to achieve. This has to be followed up with a carefully considered response which clarifies what is and what is not possible. If you are a leader in this position remember it is essential to keep the organisation's overall objectives in view at all times to keep control; at no point must you let intellectual arguments win at the expense of organisational effectiveness.

▶ *Managership and the free-rein approach.*

Managership will recognise specialist skills and abilities and will afford them the scope and freedom they need. This will be achieved by FSR so as to ensure that overall managerial control is maintained. The managership approach emphasis is: enable specialist employees to maximise their contribution to the organisation at all times.

MANAGERIAL ASSUMPTIONS AND RESPONSES

I want now to move on to considering the assumptions that lie behind the way all managers manage and lead. These assumptions may be correct and lead to appropriate management approaches and responses or they may be incorrect and lead to management and leadership problems.

Your assumptions and responses, whether correct or incorrect, are based on your perceptions of the people you have to manage and the environment in which you have to manage them. Underpinning your perceptions will be your own value system; that is, the opinions and attitudes you have evolved during the time you have spent working in organisations and as a manager. These opinions and attitudes will be, in part, based on your experiences of managing. They will either be reinforced or weakened by any new experiences to which they are exposed.

I have classified the range of possible assumptions and responses you might make into three broad groups: classical, enlightened and realistic. These classifications will enable you to consider your own assumptions and responses in the light of your organisation's actual needs, and to see if they are appropriate. Each of your managers should also review the three sets of assumptions and responses with the same objective in mind; that is, to see if it is necessary to revise some of the values and

DEVELOPMENT GUIDE 28

Managerial Assumptions and Responses

CLASSICAL: ASSUMPTIONS

(1) People are primarily motivated by money and money-related rewards; therefore money is the greatest incentive for performance that an organisation can offer.
(2) The majority of people do not willingly use their initiative and skills for the benefit of the organisations employing them.
(3) Managers are among the minority of people who use their initiative and skills for the benefit of the organisations employing them.
(4) Management's prime task in organisations is to overtly control the performance of people so that they use their skills on behalf of the organisation.
(5) The structures and systems of organisations are primarily designed to give management the maximum control over the people working in the organisation.

CLASSICAL: RESPONSES

(1) As a manager I should use money and money-related rewards primarily to get people to respond the way I want them to.
(2) As a manager I should overtly control everything my people do so that they use their skills on behalf of the organisation.
(3) Because my people will not willingly exercise initiative on behalf of the organisation I must overtly plan and organise all their work activities.
(4) As a manager I should maintain the structures and systems of the organisation so that management is both aware of, and is able to control, all the events that happen in the organisation.

ENLIGHTENED: ASSUMPTIONS

(1) There is more to working life than the acquisition of money. Many people work because it provides them with socially rewarding experiences.
(2) Technology, for many people, is reducing the opportunities for the expression of individuality and skill.
(3) The need for acceptance and to belong means that many people will covertly comply with pressures and norms generated by their peers instead of the wishes of management.
(4) People will respond positively to managements that structure work situations that enable them to meet their social as well as their economic needs.

ENLIGHTENED: RESPONSES

(1) As a manager I can improve people's performance on behalf of the organisation by making their work a more socially rewarding experience.
(2) As a manager I should consider the effects of introducing new technology on my people as well as on the organisation's balance sheet. By this approach I can plan to reduce the negative effects of the introduction of new technology.
(3) As a manager I can use peer group pressure to the advantage of the organisation. I can do this through the use of group incentives, greater group autonomy and activities such as quality circles.
(4) As a manager I can increase people's interest in their work, to the benefit of the organisation, by giving them more control over what they do and how they do it.

DEVELOPMENT GUIDE 28

Managerial Assumptions and Responses

REALISITIC: ASSUMPTIONS

(1) Given that motivated behaviour can be both intrinsically and extrinsically stimulated, a wide range of triggers should be deployed by managers to get people to perform.

(2) People have the foresight and ability to see the range of rewards available for working and will adjust their performance accordingly.

(3) People work to live rather than live to work. The quality of the life they lead is important to them: They therefore seek work that will enhance the quality of their life.

(4) Most people have a potential for further development and will welcome the opportunity to expand the range of things they can do. Developing people, therefore, increases their usefulness to the organisation.

(5) People need opportunities to express the skills and abilities they have or are developing. Organisations can benefit from giving people such opportunities.

(6) From time to time people need new challenges to stimulate them. Providing challenges is a part of the job of managing people.

(7) Given that the needs of people vary constantly, so can their performance. Management's job is to ensure that people can see their needs being fulfilled, whatever they are, by helping the organisation complete its objectives.

(8) The work place can be a source of new growth and motivational experiences for people. When people have such experiences through their work, their performance on behalf of the organisation is maximised.

REALISTIC: RESPONSES

(1) As a manager I must find ways of challenging and stimulating my people at work. This is the best way of maximising their usefulness to the organisation.

(2) Delegation is a way of committing and involving people. As a manager I should try to delegate as much as I can.

(3) As a manager I should try to make clear what I want done, how I want it done and what skills and abilities I expect will be used to do it.

(4) As a manager I need to give my people all the development opportunities they can handle sensibly. I recognise that growth increases the potential value of people to an organisation.

(5) As a manager I should try to broaden the base of decision-making in my organisation. I recognise that by increasing the decision-making powers of people I also increase their involvement with and commitment to the organisation's objectives.

(6) As a manager I should try to increase the amount of authority invested in tasks. I recognise that this will make tasks easier to complete.

opinions that underpin their approach to leading and managing.

The groupings are not mutually exclusive and both you and your managers may find that you have perceptions about people and environments which seem to cross groups. The assumptions and responses are laid out for your reference.

DISCOVERY SESSION EXERCISE

Reviewing assumptions and responses.   *Allow 40 minutes.*

 *Instructions*

When both you and your managers have read through all the assumptions and responses you should conduct an open time-out session to discuss individual feelings. This session should be kept as informal as possible to maximise the chances of people revealing their true attitudes and opinions.

LEADERSHIP: MANAGERSHIP AND THE CHIEF EXECUTIVE

Leadership is the prime activity and responsibility of the chief executive of an organisation. In most organisations it is the actions and directions of the chief executive that still largely influence what the organisation's aims, approach and philosophy are, or will be. In short, chief executives are in a better position than anyone else to make or break the organisations they head. I have already mentioned how Henry Ford's influence over his company, after stimulating its success, nearly led to its downfall; there are many more examples.

Managers and staff alike rightly or wrongly tend to look to the chief executive to set the scene and to lead them. Unfortunately, not all chief executives are prepared for the task or are even capable of doing the job.

In the film *Being There* Peter Sellers plays a person who is certainly not capable of managing or leading—a simple-minded gardener called Chance. As a result of serendipity, Chance ends up with tremendous power and influence, heading a giant corporation. The irony is that the processes of power transfer and investment portrayed in the film are not as far-fetched as they might at first appear. People are always looking for leaders who will take them to the promised land. It is because people invest so much belief in their leaders that they nearly always end up being disappointed by them. Why we ordinary mortals assume that one individual is capable of so much more than the rest of us is a mystery. It seems that we all need our gods, even if many of them turn out to have feet of clay.

REQUIREMENTS FOR THE JOB

As far as I am concerned, chief executives should first and foremost be excellent managers. They must have a track record in management which clearly indicates expensive and successful experience at all levels. Those who are promoted to chief executive with such a track record have a good change of being right for the job and therefore successful. In general, the range of skills, abilities and attributes required by the complete chief executive is considerable and it will be a rare chief executive who has them all. Your aim should be to increase your portfolio of the qualities needed for the job. The development guide which follows will help you identify which of the qualities you have or should consider developing; use it for this final exercise.

DISCOVERY EXERCISE

Identifying chief executive qualities.   *Allow 20 minutes.*

 *Instructions*

(1) Read through the chief executive's development guide list and underline in green those qualities which you consider you already possess.

(2) Read through the guide again and underline in red those qualities which you consider you most need to develop.

(3) Leave any qualities which don't fit either category for longer term reassessment.

(4) Make up two lists—qualities you have, qualities you need to develop—and get somebody who knows you well to check and modify them as necessary.

(5) When you are satisfied that you have a list for your personal development, give each quality a priority. Base this on your ability to acquire the quality as well as the need for it.

You now have the basis for a personal development plan and are in a position to consider the alternatives available for you to develop the qualities you consider you need.

Managership and the Qualities of the Chief Executive

DEVELOPMENT GUIDE 29

DECISION-MAKER

The skills, abilities and attributes needed to make decisions; to know when decisions have to be made; to make the right decisions; to, when appropriate, share the decision-making process; to enjoy the challenge of the decision-making process.

TEAM-MAKER

The skills, abilities and attributes needed to build a team; to work with a team; to work through a team; to bring out the best in each team member; to create positive synergy in a team; to recognise when a team approach is needed; to want to head up a winning team; to enjoy team leadership.

MOTIVATED-BEHAVIOUR GENERATOR

The skills, abilities and attributes needed to inspire people to respond positively; to see when people need encouragement; to respect individuality; to obtain maximum commitment; to match reward to effort; to maintain enthusiasm; to want to bring out the best in people; to inspire people; to enjoy getting people to give of their best.

SYSTEMS AND STRUCTURES SUPPORTER

The skills, abilities and attributes needed to create and build appropriate systems and structures; to work with and through systems and structures; to introduce changes in an evolutionary way; to resist change for change's sake; to be flexible but not manipulative; to respect but not sanctify systems and structures; to capitalise on the benefits of order and stability; to prevent stagnation; to prevent the means becoming the ends; to want to work with systems and structures.

VISIONARY AND STRATEGIST

The skills, abilities and attributes needed to think and act strategically; to have a vision for the future of the organisation; to convert strategies into realities; to translate strategies to operational levels successfully; to take the organisation successfully in new directions; to arrive at challenging objectives; to take the long-term view; to enjoy the challenge of dealing with the future.

COMMUNICATOR

The skills, abilities and attributes needed to communicate with all levels successfully; to communicate only when necessary; to encourage two-way communication between and across levels actively; to run an open organisation where honesty and truth are the norms; to foster positive feedback between management and workers; to enjoy communicating with all the people of the organisation.

The above list is by no means complete and you may well be able to add to it. Regardless of the composition of your final list I am confident you will find that it contains both the skills and abilities of management and the attributes needed for leadership.

In other words, managership.

CONCLUSION

The objective of the last chapter was the establishment of managership in your organisation at all levels, not just at the top. Managership is the essence of successful modern management; more than just planning, organising and controlling, management is a highly skilled activity that requires careful development. There is a lot more to running a successful organisation than charismatic leadership.

Every chapter in this book had specific objectives, each of which was aimed at improving a different aspect of managerial effectiveness. If you and your managers have realised these objectives, your organisation should soon be experiencing a payback. Your investments of time and energy, in becoming more 'hands on', will be rewarded by the achievement of the levels of managerial effectiveness you sought when you started the book.

A final word of warning—time and a continuing positive attitude will be needed to establish the long-term effectiveness you seek. You and your managers will certainly experience set-backs. Mistakes, over-enthusiasm, incorrect application and differences of opinion will occur. None of these will pose insuperable problems if your commitment to long-term effectiveness remains intact and you and your managers remain firmly 'hands on'.

Good luck

Creating the
HANDS-ON
MANAGER

═══════

APPENDIXES

═══════

APPENDIXES

CLASSIFYING MANAGEMENT ACTIVITIES: ANSWERS

General description	Activity area
(1) 'I have to carry out the one month and 12 month sales forecasts for my department and account for all the past variances.'	1
(2) 'Each month the sales office provides me with a rolling forecast of what they want. It's normally one month firm and two months flexible.'	1
(3) 'On average I attend ten meetings a month, two of which are at head office and one of which is with our main supplier.'	5
(4) 'I have thirty staff, two of whom act as my deputies. Our work is seasonal and revolves around the annual budget and accounts. I split the department down into costing and financial sections and allocate the work accordingly. It seems to work.'	4
(5) 'Part of my job is training. Each month we hold a team meeting at which two of the team are required to role-play customer situations. I provide the guidance and everyone learns something, including me.'	2
(6) 'I seem to spend half of my day on the phone chasing up missing parts for my engineers and the other half planning the work load for next week. It never goes smoothly here. The person who shouts loudest always gets priority.'	4

(7) 'I like to walk through the works at least once a day; people bring me their problems and I am able to prevent things getting out of hand. It also gets me out of the office.'

2

(8) 'My main duty is to manage the administrative assistants for the social workers in the field. I have drawn up a support rota and call regular meetings between the two groups. Before I came nobody even talked about co-operation if they could avoid it. It works better now.'

5 and 4

(9) 'When I arrived the existing staff were demoralised and staff turnover was a major problem. I couldn't pay them any more so I tried to make their working day more interesting. I plan their work schedule for the week with each member of staff and try to stick to it. Nobody has left for the last four months.'

3

MAC OVERALL SCORES

The following seven sets of sentences cover the overall scores for MAC. In some situations, particularly where traits clash, these sentences may be less accurate than the trait sentences. Even so they provide a good general guide of an overall tendency to act in a certain way. As with the individual trait sentences, underline those sentences you regard as less reliable.

SCORE BELOW 84

Will have a marked preference for working in a highly structured operating environment. A very traditional, orthodox problem-solver and decision-maker who is likely to adopt an analytical style which considers every detail. Solutions will be highly compatible with established precedents and will avoid radical approaches at all costs. Will not be pressured into responding quickly to problem situations and will seek and often demand time to adapt to change. Characterised as a rigid but dependable manager who will reject radical approaches and ideas regardless of the source.

SCORE BETWEEN 84 and 95

Problem-solving style will normally be traditional with a ready acceptance of existing constraints. Style will be characterised by a cautious approach to all new ideas and a strong wish to comply with existing proven procedures and methods. Will work at their best in a regulated operating environment with well-tried and established routines. Generally analytical with a preference for seeking out and working through all the evidence before reaching a decision. Characterised as a prudent and reliable manager who will confine problem-solving approaches to those which are supportive of the systems needed for organisational stability.

SCORE BETWEEN 96 and 106

Problem-solving style will be mainly traditional with a preference for using solutions which have been tried before. Will support new approaches on occasion as long as they are evolutionary rather than revolutionary. Unlikely to support any rapid changes of direction and will be respectful of traditional norms. Will adopt a mainly analytical approach, with decisions based on hard facts rather than intuition. Characterised as a sound and conservative manager who can be persuaded to try new routes for solving problems on occasions.

SCORE BETWEEN 107 and 136

Although an orthodox problem-solver, will not be uncomfortable with less traditional solutions if they are seen to work. Will usually seek to minimise the disruption caused by the more radical solutions offered by others. Will slow down the pace of change to allow time for assimilation. Will normally consider the organisational effects of all solutions and modify and control elements which might have adverse effects. Characterised as a conventional manager who giges due consideration both to the organisation's and to the individual's needs when solving problems.

SCORE BETWEEN 137 and 148

Problem-solving approach will incline towards the more unorthodox but still close to the mainstream. Will generally be happy seeking unusual approaches when the occasion seems to demand the same. Sees the value in change but prefers it to take an evolutionary form. Capable of separating out situations that require a creative approach from those requiring a more traditional treatment. Will be regarded by some as non-conformist but should still be able to work effectively within a traditional established organisation.

SCORE BETWEEN 148 and 169

A radical problem-solver who will seek solutions from every source regardless of organisational constraints. Enjoys challenges and working in a demanding and volatile environment as long as it allows freedom for innovative expression. Will feel constrained by too many rules and guidelines and will resist their imposition. Will have a preference for working in chunks of time rather than at a steady pace. Generally lets people get on with their assigned tasks though may take over the reins at short notice. Characterised as an erractic and slightly unstable manager whose effectiveness as a problem-solver will be constantly questioned.

SCORE
ABOVE 169

A lateral thinker who is naturally inclined to adopt radical and often unique solutions. Has almost no regard for established precedents or organisational compliance. Will always adopt new methods even when traditional approaches may be strongly recommended. Will make great steps forward and then over-react. Likely to experience many dead ends. Will have a strong preference for working free of supervision. Will resent criticism and be regarded by many as unstable and lacking in rational judgement. Will find it difficult to fit into the majority of traditional organisations. Supervised staff will have to be able to work with the minimum of direction. Characterised as a highly unpredictable manager with a very radical approach to problem-solving.

MAC TESTS AND SCORES

Below you will find a set of sentences for each of the three traits assessed by MAC. Use the scores you achieved for each of the traits to arrive at the set of sentences that matches your score for each trait. It may be that you do not agree with all of the sentences. If so, underline those which you feel are less appropriate.

MAC TRAIT: INNOVATIVE DISPOSITION

SCORES
UNDER 28

Will always try to solve problems using tried and tested methods. Will dislike changes that alter existing working arrangements. Likely to treat most new ideas with suspicion and consider them a threat to the established order. Inclined to accept long-term problems as constraints that have to be worked with. Will not like risking doing things differently even in a crisis. Usually prefers to tackle problems one at a time in the order they are received. Will expect team members to solve problems within given detailed instructions.

<table>
<tr><td>

SCORES
BETWEEN
28 and 34

</td><td>

Will tackle problems in a planned and ordered manner. Will rarely act on own initiative, preferring to work within established procedures for problem-solving and decision-making. Most ideas and solutions will stem from proven methods and be designed so as to fit in with existing norms. Will seek to restrict staff problem-solving initiatives to ensure that the solutions generated are not too radical or disruptive to the organisation. Likely to resist all suggestions for change that are of a radical nature unless the evidence and support for the change is overwhelming.

</td></tr>
<tr><td>

SCORES
BETWEEN
35 and 49

</td><td>

Generally will prefer the established way of doing things, but will try new ways given sufficient supporting evidence. On occasion will generate new ideas and solutions; however, most initiatives will be based on traditional concepts. If pressed to do so, will be capable of tackling several problems at once, but will seek to limit the number of problems needing attention at any one time. Will allow team members the freedom to tackle assignments in their own way as long as the 'rules' are observed.

</td></tr>
<tr><td>

SCORES
BETWEEN
50 and 56

</td><td>

Will usually risk doing things differently if by doing so a problem can be solved. Will accept most changes that are perceived as supportive of positive progress; will be more resistant to changes that seek to restrict personal initiatives. Ideas and solutions will often have an original quality and change the established way of doing things. Will be prepared to tackle several different problems at the same time and will change priorities at short notice. Will allow team members considerable scope in the way they tackle problems; sometimes this may lead to confusion and disruption.

</td></tr>
<tr><td>

SCORES
OVER 56

</td><td>

A lateral thinker stimulated by tasks requiring unique solutions or new approaches. Will have a strong preference for working on own initiative and will feel restricted by most overt organisational policies and procedures. Likely to enjoy coping with several problems at the same time although inclined to lose interest quickly if no positive feedback received. Will not feel constrained by established methods, norms or rules and will tend to ignore them when solving problems or planning future events. Will give team members many opportunities for free expression when they are problem solving regardless of organisational requirements to conform. Will be regarded by many as a disruptive and unstable influence within the organisation.

</td></tr>
</table>

MAC TRAIT: ORGANISATIONAL COMPLIANCE

SCORES
BELOW 28

Will place a high priority on observing the rules and following laid down policies. Will never act without authority and will seek the approval of seniors for all important actions. Will have a strong preference for working in a structured and ordered operating environment where everyone knows the limitations of their authority. Will resist suggestions for radical change from colleagues and will always support the established organisation.

SCORES
BETWEEN
28 and 34

Will see the reasoning behind adherence to bureaucratic structures and the general need to conform. Will nearly always follow the set policy and avoid stepping outside the established way. Will inform seniors of all key decisions and will seek their advice on all major courses of action. Will expect to be well briefed by seniors on all tasks. Will endeavour to see that organisational needs have priority at all times.

SCORES
BETWEEN
35 and 49

Will usually see the need to follow organisational policies and rules but may become frustrated on occasions. Will try to introduce changes when it is proved that they are really necessary. Will normally be comfortable in a bureaucratic environment as long as personal goals and objectives are being achieved. Will consider the views and needs of staff when working towards organisational objectives. Generally has a liking for the stability found in well-established organisations.

SCORES
BETWEEN
50 and 56

Will often find organisational policies and procedures inhibiting. Will not be afraid to challenge and question higher authority. Actions will not always be seen as consistent and will display a preference for adjusting approaches to suit different problem situations. Will normally refer decisions to higher authority when asked to do so or when their 'own' solution is certain to be accepted. Normally willing to break rules in pursuit of objectives. Will allow staff considerable freedom to make decisions and solve problems until they are proved to be unreliable at doing so.

SCORES
OVER 56

Tendency to ignore policies, norms and rules in the pursuit of objectives. Will change the operating environment to suit specific situations. Generally finds systems and procedures very restricting and is highly frustrated by having to comply with them. Shows little or no respect for higher authority unless the individuals concerned have qualities they admire. Usually a square peg in a round hole in a bureaucracy of any kind.

MAC TRAIT: OCCUPATIONAL PREOCCUPATION

SCORES BELOW 28

Will meticulously check every detail to ensure it is correct. Will need to have all the information to hand before making a decision or taking any action. Plans very carefully all day-to-day routines. Needs to work in a 'logical' sequence and will be unsettled by rapid changes of priority. Will show a marked reluctance to delegate important tasks and will require detailed feedback on all delegated tasks from subordinates.

SCORES BETWEEN 28 and 34

Will work in an ordered and systematic way, taking care to ensure there are no loose ends. Will feel more secure making decisions based on detailed supporting evidence. Will work at a steady pace with a capacity to spend long periods of time on single tasks. Likes to use memos and reports to keep self well informed about what is going on. Will frequently use meetings to check on how staff are performing and on how tasks are progressing.

SCORES BETWEEN 35 and 49

Will have a preference for checking details personally but will trust others to do so on occasions. Will occasionally make decisions without supporting evidence but will expect most requests for action and attention to be well backed up. Will approach most tasks in a consistent and methodical way and will resist attempts to rush ahead. Normally willing to delegate key tasks, controlling progress by issuing detailed instructions.

SCORES BETWEEN 50 and 56

Inclined to use intuition as well as evidence when making decisions. Will normally find checking details a problem and on occasion will miss obvious errors. Work routines and patterns will lack consistency but will contain periods of inspired activity. Will prefer to exercise 'exception' controls over staff, allowing them to find their own routes to task completion. Will approach given problems from several broad angles, preferring to consider the total picture rather than get locked into the detail. Will normally only consider the detail when forced to do so.

SCORES OVER 56

Decision-making will be of a radical nature. Will tend to ignore the detailed considerations when attempting to achieve the overall objectives. Will enjoy problem-solving more than routine work and will be inclined to seek out interesting problems to tackle rather than get involved in the daily routine. Will not have any discernable work patterns and may 'opt out' for a time then undergo a period of rapid desk clearing. Very willing to delegate important tasks without detailed instructions unless they are requested.

MATE TESTS AND SCORES

Below you will find a set of sentences, each of which describes a different level of effective managerial thinking ability. As MATE is an aptitude assessment some of the sets of sentences describe weaknesses and some describe strengths. To avoid negative effects great care must be taken to ensure that the scores on the assessment are matched to the right set of sentences.

MATE can be used for recruitment as well as development purposes. In either case care must also be taken when feeding back results. Effective thinking ability can be considerably improved and therefore a poor result should not be taken as a signal for writing someone off. Most good management development programmes will increase effective thinking ability.

LESS THAN OR EQUAL TO 24	Likely to have a very poor overall ability to think effectively. Has not really demonstrated any aptitude for effective managerial thinking. Scores of this level are not normally found amongst management populations and may indicate a language or concept understanding problem. If other measures indicate satisfactory thinking skills, re-assess.
SCORES BETWEEN 25 and 33 INCLUSIVE	Effective managerial thinking ability likely to be well below average. Will be inclined to be too trusting and easily misled. Unlikely to be able to differentiate between conflicting arguments and may miss important assumptions. Will not appear to be confident when making decisions and may be regarded as indecisive. Scores of this level indicate a need for substantial effective thinking development.
SCORES BETWEEN 34 and 41 INCLUSIVE	Effective managerial thinking ability is below average and needs to be improved. Will be inclined to make too many wrong decisions and will not always fully appreciate underlying assumptions or the differing values in arguments. Could find decision-making in situations of ambiguity a particular problem. Scores of this level indicate a need for an ongoing development of effective thinking ability.

SCORES BETWEEN 42 and 48 INCLUSIVE	In general the level of effective managerial thinking ability is acceptable. Scores at the lower end of the range suggest that effective thinking needs sharpening. On most occasions should be able to recognise implied assumptions although convoluted arguments may cause confusion. Scores of this level may indicate that the manager concerned is in a position that does not demand too much decision-making. Make allowances for such situations. Should be able to improve effective thinking ability with training.
SCORES BETWEEN 49 and 56 INCLUSIVE	Effective managerial thinking ability is average or just above. Scores at the upper end of this range suggest that effective thinking is reasonably sharp. Will be able to recognise the day-to-day assumptions people make and weigh the strength of arguments. Likely to demonstrate reasonable analysis and evaluation skills. Should be able to handle abstract concepts without too much difficulty. Scores of this level suggest that maintenance development and training would be appropriate to both sustain and improve effective thinking performance.
SCORES BETWEEN 57 and 64 INCLUSIVE	Good effective thinking ability with an aptitude for decision-making. Should, as long as personality factors are acceptable, be able to handle day-to-day problem-solving and decision-making at a number of management levels. Scores of this level indicate a good all-round thinking ability which may well be capable of further development.
SCORES BETWEEN 65 and 73 INCLUSIVE	An above average effective managerial thinker. Likely to be able to handle a wide range of problem-solving and decision-making situations. Will normally cope with ambiguity and lack of comprehensive information. Will take abstract concepts in their stride. Should be able to think through strategic as well as operational decision processes. Scores of this level indicate that little additional effective thinking development is required. Personality assessment results should be assessed to establish communication skills and overall potential.
SCORES GREATER THAN OR EQUAL TO 74	A first-class effective managerial thinker. Will be able to cope with the most obscure assumptions, inferences and arguments. Will have no problem handling all forms of problem analysis. Should be able to think strategically as well as operationally. Scores in this range indicate a very high level of abstract thinking ability. Personality assessment results should be assessed to establish ability to relate to other people and communicate with those of lesser ability.

REFERENCES AND ADDRESSES

————————PUBLICATIONS————————

Belbin, R.M. (1981). *Management Teams: Why They Succeed or Fail.* London: Heinemann.

Cattell, R.B. *et al.* (1970). *Handbook for the Sixteen Personality Factor Questionnaire (16PF).* Champaign, Illinois: IPAT Inc.

Karson, S., and O'Dell (1976). *Clinical Use of 16PF.* Champaign, Illinois: IPAT Inc.

Krug, S. (1981). *Interpreting 16PF Profiles Patterns.* Champaign, Illinois: IPAT Inc.

Machiavelli, N. *The Prince.* London: Dent, Everyman's Library.

Margerison, C.J., and McCann, D.J. (1984). *Team Management Index.* MCB University Press.

Mintzberg, H. (1973). *The Nature of Managerial Work.* San Francisco: Harper and Row.

Wang, An. (1986). *Lessons.* Addison-Wesley Publishing Co.

————————VIDEO/FILMS————————

Time to Think (1985 version) Rank Audio Visual

Meetings Bloody Meetings Video Arts

More Bloody Meetings Video Arts

————————ADDRESSES————————

NFER-Nelson Publishing Co. Ltd.
Darville House, 2 Oxford Road East, Windsor, Berkshire SL4 1DF.
Main publisher/distributor and exclusive agent for the sale and distribution of 16PF materials in the UK.

Independent Assessment and Research Centre
57 Marylebone High Street, London W1M 3AE.
UK provider of the pcdp.

The Test Agency Ltd.
Cournswood House, North Dean, High Wycombe, Bucks, HP14 4NW.
16PF approved training.

THE HANDS-ON MANAGER FOLLOW-UP SERVICE

The Test Agency have agreed to provide a follow-up service for MAC and MATE materials. This service will enable you to purchase direct from the Test Agency purpose designed copies of MAC and MATE.

▶ THE INITIAL MAC PACKAGE ◀ INCLUDES:

(1) 50 self-marking response sheets.
(2) 50 research data information sheets.
(3) A computer disk [plus two back-up copies] containing a comprehensive program that will enable you to generate individual reports, create a database and analyse the collected data. The program also contains an on-line help facility.
(4) A simple instruction manual that tells you how to administer, score and generally use MAC successfully.

▶ THE INITIAL MATE PACKAGE ◀ INCLUDES:

(1) 50 times four sets of self-marking response sheets.
(2) 50 research data information sheets.
(3) 20 participant manuals with examples of how to respond to the questions in MATE.
(4) A computer disk [plus two back-up copies] containing a comprehensive program that will enable you to generate individual reports and recommendations, create a database and analyse the collected data. The program also contains an on-line help facility.
(5) A simple instruction manual that tells you how to administer, score and generally use MATE successfully.

You can purchase these packages separately or as a set. After you have acquired the initial package or packages you will be able to purchase additional sets of response sheets separately.
For more information and prices contact:

Phyllis or David Morgan
The Test Agency Ltd.
Cournswood House, North Dean, High Wycombe, Bucks HP14 4NW.
Tel: Naphill (024-024) 3384; Telex: 837549 ARPECO.G; Fax: Naphill (024-024) 3382.